Fundamentally Female

by Reneé Rongen

Edited by
Carol McAdoo Rehme

Graphic Design by
Annette Wood

Kittleson Creek PRESS

Kittleson Creek Press
10601 390th St. SE
Fertile, MN 56540

Fundamentally Female™ is a trademark of Reneé Rongen & Associates, LLC.

Printed in Canada.

Visit www.reneerongen.com for links to contributors.

Library of Congress Control Number: 2012915410

ISBN: 978-0-9881856-0-9

Dedicated to
The Birthday Club
Thank you for always believing in me, encouraging me, and disciplining me!

RWR

ONE
DAY
IT
WAS
SUDDENLY
REVEALED
TO
ME
THAT
EVERYTHING
IS
PURE
SPIRIT.

RADAKRISHNA

A woman with spirit sparkles when she walks into a room. She has eyes that smile and a smile that catches eyes. Her inner beauty far outshines her surface beauty.

She fully embraces every experience as a mission-in-the-moment. Glowing with her love for life, a woman with spirit shares her joy with all those she touches.

Shari L. Fruechte

up front

Perhaps I made the discovery while sitting at the feet of my 103-year-old great-grandmother over high tea, or maybe when I slipped out my bedroom window as a teenager to escape with my girlfriends, or possibly when I eavesdropped on the conversations of the ladies in my mother's Birthday Club. Somehow, somewhere, I knew I had a hunger for the way women navigated the world.

I knew we talked differently than males, more curious about the inner workings of the soul than the mechanisms of a car. I understood that women would much rather give a detailed account of childbirth and read steamy romances or self-help books than comprehend the full operating instructions for a food processor. As I matured and accumulated life experiences, I became even more convinced that we as women are not like our testosterone-laden counterparts.

This is not a man-bashing book. I adore men! (Ask all my old boyfriends.) This book simply celebrates the essence, the spirit of women. We are, in a sense, our own club. We are mothers, daughters, sisters, grandmothers, friends. We share a bond, a sisterhood of similar experiences and emotions.

My desire to compile this book was born out of a certainty that women share more commonalities than differences. Thankfully, others caught my vision and grasped my concept. They embraced the project with enthusiasm and creativity, adding new flavors with surprising ingredients.

As a result, this global concoction—for, about, and largely by women—identifies our universal soul: the friendships we honor, the vulnerability we expose, the impact we make, the intimacy we covet, the secrets we keep. Rich in wit and wisdom, humor and honesty, this collection of candid and diverse voices speaks to generations of females in search of confirmation. And inspiration.

Although the women within these pages have names different than yours, I believe you will see a reflection of yourself in their offerings. Their stories are candid. Their quips are honest. Their eclectic artwork is multi-dimensional. Like colorful tiles, their individual pieces complete an intricate mosaic—a whole as complex and contradictory as the women who created them.

Within the folds of these covers, may you discover pieces of yourself. You might shout your acknowledgement or giggle your agreement. You might even shed a healing tear or two. Above all, I hope you, too, nod in agreement at the universal characteristics, the common traits, that make us all, every single one of us... fundamentally female.

RWR

Reneé Wall Rongen

hot [hot]

adjective, hot·ter, hot·test,
adverb, verb, hot·ted, hot·ting,
noun adjective
1. having or giving off heat; having a
high temperature: a hot fire; hot coffee.
2. having or causing a sensation of great
bodily heat; attended with or producing
such a sensation: He was hot with fever.
3. creating a burning sensation, as on th
ski------ -a th---- This --- -tment is -

Growing up in rural America had many advantages. My favorite was you knew everyone in your hometown and they knew you. Of course, that could also be the biggest disadvantage: Sometimes they knew what you did even before you did it! At a recent class reunion, I reminisced with old friends, recounting tale after tale from our childhoods. My chuckles turned to side splitting laughter and, before long, I was worried that the latest small town rumor on the street would relate how Reneé Rongen laughed so hard that tears ran down her legs.

> *"Don't be dismayed at goodbyes. A farewell is necessary before you can meet again. And meeting again, after moments or lifetimes, is certain for those who are friends."*
>
> Richard Bach

It is the morning after my thirtieth class reunion. Wow! If I ever had a self-esteem problem—which I don't think I have—it certainly would have been rectified over the weekend.

As a student at a small school in Northwestern Minnesota, I knew everyone in my class; I floated from group to group, friends with most everyone. Those friends from my childhood have rooted me, believed in me, and so many times been my source of inspiration for writing and speaking. It is no surprise that they kept me grounded and true to myself. The endearing phrase of the weekend was, "Have I told you in the last hour how *hot* you are?" Men and women approaching middle age made the same comment to each other. It wasn't a sexual innuendo. It was a term of endearment.

Never before have I been told so many times by so many people how loved I was. The kind of love that says, *I know all of you: your hopes, your dreams, your fears. And I share in your joy, laughter, and triumphs.* There was no need for pretending that life is something greater or less than what it is, because these friends have traveled my journey and they really do know me.

They made me feel so complete and safe in my own skin. The surreal weekend seemed straight from a movie screen, one long "Big Chill" kind of moment.

I have a lighter step this morning and a perpetual smile on my face as I picture us all dancing to "Greased Lightning" and laughing out loud when we pushed someone to the middle and danced around them. Although my knees are not reflecting the smile on my face, it is a small price to pay for so much fun and nostalgia. As I tow the vacuum and dust the furniture, no one runs up to hug and squeeze me, but—in my heart—I'm know I'm still *hot*!

RWR

> "The externals are simply so many props; everything we need is within us."
>
> Etty Hillesum

Kicking
the
Crap
out of
Cancer

"You have cancer."

The doctor's words stunned me. I had cancer? Incurable, he explained, but controllable.

The first step in my treatment involved then-experimental drugs. We watched. We waited. Finally, as the cancer progressed, I committed to a stem cell transplant. Gathering my wits, I made plans for an eleven-week stay at the Mayo clinic in Rochester, Minnesota. But I would need someone with me twenty-four hours a day.

I called my younger sister. "Can you help me?"

Without hesitating, Jody replied, "Where? And when?"

My second and third calls went to longtime friends who live near Rochester. "Can you help me?"

"Where?" asked Gretchen.

"When?" asked Gladys.

No checking schedules, no excuses about family commitments. Eager to help, all three women generously put their own lives on hold in order to save mine.

Between them, these three beautiful, dedicated—and sometimes tough—ladies got me up and going every morning. They tucked me into bed every night. They created a daily ritual for me and a support system for my husband, a team effort that lasted nearly three months.

Doctors pronounced the stem cell transplant a success. But I know the *real* success was achieved through the strength and dedication of a trio of angels who held me when I cried, who teased me until I laughed, who bullied me when I wanted to give up. Women who gave me three more reasons to hope.

Sharon Wall

constant

pliant

Her eyes tell a thousand stories of a life well lived.

They tell of a young farm girl, working like a man but yearning for girlish things. Of a girl with so many dreams, who willingly surrendered to life and embraced it with gusto.

She did not become a famous actress on Broadway; she starred in community theater productions for four decades. She did not become a nurse; she worked as a home health aide, earning minimum wages bathing, changing bandages, checking meds, and warming soup for the sick, the homebound, and the lonely. She did not become a famous singer; she participated in the church choir for fifty years and cherished her night out to attend rehearsals once a week.

At eighty-one, she lives fully, continuing to inspire and nurture. She bakes cakes for funerals, nurses her aging friends, and loves her children and grandchildren. She even makes a little extra cash riding with the sheriff to transport female prisoners across the state. She looks at those young women with her experienced eyes and tells them to be good. To pray.

Acceptance. No regrets. The challenge is making the choice to be happy with what we have. The challenge is living our simple lives in a world that emphasizes glamour and fame. The challenge is to live it well.

Our eyes will tell the story.

Marsha Miller

One winter while I was in college, an Explorer Scout leader and friend convinced me to go hiking in the Grand Canyon. With packs on our backs, crampons on our shoes, and ski poles in our hands, we trekked down the unmaintained Tanner Trail.

A timid New Jersey transplant, I braved narrow, icy paths near the rim. I confronted unfenced, sheer drops of thousands of feet. First crawling to those yawning precipices on my hands and knees, I quickly adapted and stood upright—to face, head-on, my fears of the unknown and my dread of heights.

The lesson? Don't let fear stand in the way of a good adventure. Instead, use the fear, transform it, and celebrate your willingness to face "grand" new experiences!

Andrea H. Gold

You can run out of unclimbed peaks. But if you're creative, you'll never run out of adventures.

Nancy Feagin

nostalgic

She remembers the simple joy of jump rope, hopscotch, and Easy Bake Ovens. She remembers playing dress-up and the thrill of stepping into Mommy's high heels. She remembers the special teacher who helped her when she needed it most. She remembers her first crush and signing his name with x's and o's. She remembers her first kiss and her first heartbreak. She remembers her friends and family and all they taught her. She remembers the big decisions she made and knows they make her what she is today. She knows there is no regret, only lessons. She knows there is value in the remembering.

Tammy Tobin

confounding

Aerodynamically—due to its tiny wings and heavy body—the bumblebee shouldn't be able to fly. But no one told the bumblebee, so it flies anyway. Every woman who succeeds in the face of adversity is un-BEE-table.

Carol McAdoo Rehme

When I look at the women who have been part of my inner circle, I define their commonalities. They are Truth Tellers. They have strong personalities coupled with warm hearts and a desire to grow to become more than who they are now. Self-revelatory, they are good conversationalists, powerfully committed to their marriages, children, families, and friends. They are women of humor and creativity. And they have a fierce and steadfast love of God, open to His work in their lives.

They influence me and teach me things like:

Acceptance, knowing you are safe to say the ugly things in your head and will not be judged. Laughed at, maybe, but never judged.

Loyalty, meaning if you hurt my friend you hurt me. When your life implodes and you are on the evening news, they insist the camera didn't make you look fat.

Truth, when it is flattering and when it is not.

Hope, regardless of how bad life looks or feels. These women can and will find the lesson to be learned, the character trait to be developed, or the spiritual truth that brings life to any hopeless moment.

Laughter, especially when there's no counsel for the current calamity. They always, always find a kernel of humor. The kind that catches you off guard, a reminder that you've survived other miseries and you will survive this one, too.

Lord knows, I could not have survived church politics or teacher's meetings without my friends. Every life experience has been richer, deeper, and sweeter because of the women who walked me through them.

Kim Clements

supportive

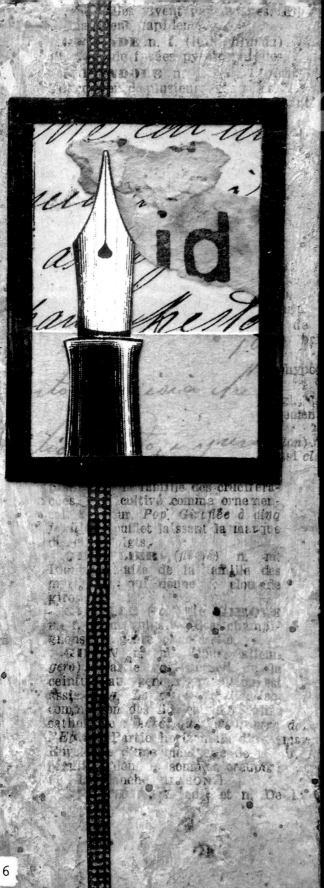

> **Forgiveness is giving up the hope that the past could have been any different.**
>
> Oprah Winfrey

flexible

No single term seems to encompass all that I am. The woman I thought I was, the woman I hoped to become, is far afield from where I have landed. But I am not finished. My race is not over. My spirit, that supernatural piece that ultimately defines who I am, gives me the capacity to make those decisions.

And I know for certain that my spirit is a prism.

My prism reflects all of the elements comprising me. My beauty and strife as a mother is sometimes golden, sometimes fire-red, sometimes the deepest blue. My prism reflects the shades of me as a lawyer, the shades of me in love, the shades of my desires, each with its own vivid color wheel.

My life today is very different from my life even four years ago. I went through a painful divorce and the process of healing. Dead inside, I was able to meet only the most basic needs of my children. My prism was dark, colorless.

But slowly, my spirit opened to healing and grace. I resurfaced. Me. Not in an inappropriate and selfish way, but with dignity, beauty, love, and strength.

"Whatever doesn't kill you makes you stronger," some say.

I say, "Whatever doesn't kill you makes you smarter."

Strength, I've learned, is part of my spirit — if it's allowed to surface. I can't rewrite where I've been, but I can start a bright, light, new chapter.

Lisa McLeod-Lofquist

positive

> "A woman is the full circle.
> Within her is the power to create,
> nurture and transform."
>
> Diane Marie Child

Donna Mae Carlson was The Krumkake Queen.

Each year, I placed a large order for her culinary delicacies: forty dozen at Thanksgiving and another forty dozen at Christmas. I delighted in taking her tender Norwegian cookies to exchanges and family feasts. And I always shared the story of the special little woman who made them.

Donna expressed her love for her family and friends by baking and took pleasure in the tedious creation of her krumkake. At more than eighty-years-old, she was going strong despite arthritis that deformed her fingers and hands, making each crisp little roll of sugar and flour and cream a miracle. Lovingly stowed in shoeboxes, carefully wrapped in paper towels, the krumkake symbolized her joy in the art of making and doing.

Our Krumkake Queen passed away two days ago. I know all the angels in heaven will love her baking, too!

Dr. Susan Mathison

able

"Together we have a voice!"
Folashade Oni, age 16

united

When I hear someone say, "Be yourself," I think shorts and tights. I guess being myself has never been too hard for me. Be it funky earrings, crazy up-dos, or just an outfit that no one gets but me, I've always had fun doing my own thing. I don't know if I'm an artist or an eccentric, but at least I have fun. So, I am okay with being out of the box. There's more room to be myself.

Quin R. Hasler, age 13

"Be adventurous. Try a lot of different things. Who cares doesn't work out? It's only

Mary Eng

proud

Our lives forever changed the day she entered it; now she's ready to tackle the universe. My first-born daughter is preparing to leave high school and begin college. When does she stop being our baby girl? On graduation day? Her wedding day? When she becomes a parent herself? Never. I used to believe my job was to help her mature into a woman. Now, I'm grateful for the maturity this spectacular young woman developed in *me*. I have progressed from trying to sculpt her into my vision, to standing in awe of the masterpiece of which God has appointed me curator for the past eighteen years. Admiration replaces frustration for the strong, feisty, independent, and sincere spirit she exudes. Watch out world—she's on her way!

Leah Burke

deluded

He shuffled down the street today
a boyfriend of mine
four decades back.
Marshmallow waist, shining
pate. Father Time had charcoaled
the black.

His eyes met mine.
Startled, amused, I
flirted, winked, sashayed
away.

Trailing a lilting laugh like
wafting perfume,
I left him standing there.
Curious, confused,
surely pining the shapely
young lass teasing
his memory today.

Carol McAdoo Rehme

resilient

"A childhood of abuse and torture birthed within me a victorious spirit. My challenges taught me compassion, kindness, and forgiveness. In spite of broken wings, I choose to soar.

Momma Joyce Lest

Feet, what do I need you for when I have wings to fly?

— Frida Kahlo

optimistic

My legs are long stilts.

They are usually bruised from all the basketball and volleyball I play. They lead down to my narrow, size eleven feet, which have always embarrassed me. Now that I'm finally growing into my feet, I realize they were just an indicator that the rest of me would catch up. I'm fourteen and have grown five inches in less than two years, topping out at 5'9". And I'm still growing!

I'm able to laugh when friends comment on the length of my feet. The only problem? I love to shop and, other than athletic footwear, there sure isn't much of a selection in my size. Maybe I'll be a shoe designer when I grow up!

Grace Rongen, age 14

Best friends

fortunate

You are blessed if you have
even one special woman friend
in your life. A woman listens.
She cares. And she puts her
arms around you.

Collette Conati

selfless

One hundred little babies lay three and four to a cardboard box, strapped in the belly of a gutted cargo jet. It was 1975, Saigon was falling to the Communists, and I was accidentally caught up in the Vietnam Orphan Airlift. Today, as a sixty-two-year-old grandma, I still shake my head in wonder.

All I intended to do was buy a dozen cupcakes.

It all started when I was a little girl living a frugal, happy life on our Iowa farm. Mom and Dad taught their eight children to eat their broccoli because kids in Korea were starving. We donated our hand-me-downs to the Thanksgiving clothing drives at church. We trick-or-treated for UNICEF and learned that two-and-a-half cents could buy a carton of milk and save a child's life. That's when I began to believe we *are* called to be our brother's keeper, to share all we've been given. I decided I'd adopt an orphan someday. So certain was I, that I shared that dream during the romantic moment Mark asked me to marry him. Then it became our dream.

It was all of these things that led me to stop that day as I pushed the stroller and our two little girls to the bake sale booth at the mall. The cupcakes sat beneath the poster of a

starving child and a sign that read Friends of Children of Vietnam. I wanted to help. To make a difference. So I bought a dozen cupcakes. And became a member … and then the president … and my basement became the Iowa chapter headquarters of FCVN. We handful of young moms raised food, money, supplies, and awareness for the orphans in Vietnam, shipping five tons of supplies in three years.

Then the national officers asked the fateful question—would I be the next escort to bring six adopted babies back to their assigned families in the States? It was the toughest decision of my life. I considered that Mark and I had applied for adoption of a son through FCVN, with two more years to wait. There had been no increase in the war in months and daily calls to the State Department assured me the fighting was far from Saigon, not expected to escalate. I'd be safe.

So I agreed to go.

By the time I arrived there was a tremendous Viet Cong offensive. Bombs were exploding outside the city, and I was greeted with, "Have you heard the news? President Ford okayed Operation Babylift. You won't be taking out six babies, but 300!"

I entered the FCVN orphanage center to find hundreds of babbling, bawling babies. Every inch of floor was covered with a mat and every inch of mat was covered with a baby. We spent day and night caring for them, naming them, and preparing them for evacuation.

On the second day, I entered the warehouse to pack for three hundred babies. Imagine how I felt when I brushed dust from the top of a box and saw my own handwriting! We had shipped this box from my basement just the month before. Now I was packing the clothes again … sending them back to the States … this time on a baby going to a new home.

My assignment the third day nearly stopped my heart. I could walk into the next room and choose a son. Incredibly, in the midst of the chaos, a baby boy crawled across the room into my arms, my heart, and our family. He chose me.

Gunfire, bombs, explosions, and government delays stalled Operation Babylift. But on day five, with my own son in tow, I helped load hundreds of babies into open cardboard boxes strapped to the floor of a cargo jet where they finally flew to freedom and families.

For the next twenty years I loved my life as a full-time mom and a part-time nurse, raising our three children with Mark. We encouraged them to eat their vegetables because the kids in Vietnam were starving, and to donate their hand-me-downs, time, and portions of their allowances to the needy.

Finally, as our "baby boy" left for college, I began to write our story. After five years and twenty-one rejections, I sold my book, *This Must Be My Brother*. A national nursing organization asked if I would speak at their state conference. Who me? Speak? On what? "Tell us what you learned from Operation Babylift," they coaxed. That was the start of my prolific speaking and writing career.

All this, from buying a dozen cupcakes.

LeAnn Thieman

wise [wahyz]

adjective, wis·er, wis·est, verb, wised, wis·ing
1. having the power of discerning and judging properly as to what is true or right; possessing discernment, judgment, or dis...

Find the perfect husband.

There it was, right on my to-do list. As a strong-willed woman, I knew this would not be an easy task. I had dated some really terrific men, but none of them was a match for my soul.

"Honey," my mom said, "God will bring you the right man when you are least suspecting."

Like I hadn't heard that a thousand times before. "But how will I know?"

"He will be tender. Find a man who thinks his mother hung the moon. He will love you the same way, and he will love the Lord!"

Mom was right. I was twenty-eight when my husband proposed—after he flew to meet with my parents and ask for my hand in marriage.

wise

I walked in the back door of my in-laws' house like I had hundreds of times before. I stepped over untied tennis shoes and work boots before landing in the kitchen long enough to set the newest medical bills on the counter next to the bin of Loracet, Prednisone, and Tylox bottles.

Down the hall, my mother-in-law lay in a hospital bed in what had previously been the sewing room. Startled to hear bedrails grate and drop from their upright position, I raced toward her room. But giggles stopped me in my tracks.

Giggling? Who was with her? I knew her fulltime nurse was charting in the nearby office. So who was tending to my mother-in-law?

I took another step and put my ear to the crack of the partially opened door. The next laugh was my husband's. I was about to announce my presence when I heard Tom say, "This ain't nothing, Mom. At least you don't squirm around and throw your legs over your head like Elizabeth." Clearly, Tom was describing our toddler's routine diaper change.

What a happy and holy fashion it is

that those who love one another should rest on the same pillow.

"Now, Mom, do you want a firm and snug fit or do you think you want it looser?"

"Oh you better give me the firm and snug fit." She might be fighting for dignity, but she hadn't lost her sense of humor. "You never know when I am going to bound out of this bed and begin my callisthenic routine!"

> **Love never gives up, never loses faith, is always hopeful, and endures through every circumstance.**
>
> I Corinthians 13:7

I smiled to myself at the familiar banter between them, their way of masking the unbearable truth. Tom's fifty-eight-year-old mother, once so vibrant and beautiful, wore a crooked yellow and black turban and a body swollen to twice its size by high doses of Prednisone and high-potency cancer cocktails.

Silence penetrated the room. I pressed my ear closer. Was she fatigued from her adult-diaper change? Just as I started to tiptoe in, she spoke in her quiet way.

"Son, you make me laugh when I should be red with embarrassment. I am so proud of the man you have become. Your father would have been, too. Thank you for taking such good care of me." Her voice as faint as a whisper, she asked, "Pray with me?"

Shamelessly, barely suppressing my tears, I listened as this dear woman thanked God for life, for laughter, and for the gift of her son. "I know all things are possible through You," she added. "Amen."

I nudged the door open in time to see my husband kiss the woman who had given him life and encouraged him to live it.

"I love you, Mom," he murmured into her ear.

"I know." She mouthed the words as her sunken eyes drifted shut. "I know."

impudent

Beauty is in the eye of the beholder, and it may be necessary from time to time to give a stupid or misinformed beholder a black eye.

Miss Piggy

thoughtful

On one of my first shifts as a student intern in a nursing home, I ran into difficulty. My patient, a severely disabled young man who couldn't speak or move his limbs, required extensive care. When I struggled to get a blood pressure cuff on his arm, I asked my instructor, Nancy, for help.

I observed as, with practiced ease, she performed morning duties on my patient. She engaged him with a wonderfully conversational tone, speaking as if they were having a good chat. Watching her with alert eyes, the man smiled, made small nods, and tried to move his head to see her.

When Nancy noticed his chapped lips, she picked up the stick of lip ointment from his nightstand. Tenderly, taking her time, she applied it, first to the upper, then the lower, coating his dry lips with the soothing balm.

Only his eyes could express his relief and gratitude. It was Nancy who spoke. "Thank you." She touched his foot. "Thank you for letting us serve you."

Maureen J. Andrade

Recently, my fourteen-year-old daughter burst into tears and asked why her birth mother gave her away. *You have me, I wanted to say. Don't be sad. I am your mom now. Isn't that good enough?*

But I didn't say any of those things. I wanted so desperately to take away her pain. Somehow, I found the strength in the moment to be His face, His voice, to let Him handle this through me.

"I know you're sad," I heard myself say, instead. "Tell me more about how you feel."

And He put His arms around her to … simply … listen.

Marsha Miller

humble

> **"Learn to be quiet enough to hear the genuine within yourself so that you can hear it in others."**
> Marian Wright Edelman

silent

MY GRANDMOTHER WAS ALWAYS SILENT—ALWAYS AGGRIEVED—ONLY HER HUSBAND HAD THE COSMIC RIGHT (OR SO IT WAS SAID) TO SPEAK AND BE HEARD. TOO MANY WOMEN IN TOO MANY COUNTRIES SPEAK THE SAME LANGUAGE OF SILENCE. MY GRANDMOTHER THINKS I TALK TOO MUCH). BUT SOMETIMES I WONDER. WHEN A WOMAN FIGHTS FOR POWER, AS MOST DO GENEROUSLY—IT IS ACCEPTED. WHEN A WOMAN SHARES HER THOUGHTS, AS SOME DO GRACIOUSLY, IT IS ALLOWED. WHEN A WOMAN GIVES HER LOVE, AS ALL WOMEN WOULD LIKE TO, QUIETLY OR LOUDLY, IT IS QUESTIONED. AND YET, THERE MUST BE FREEDOM—IF WE ARE TO SPEAK, AND YES, THERE MUST BE POWER—IF WE ARE TO BE HEARD, AND WHEN WE HAVE BOTH FREEDOM AND POWER—LET US NOT BE MISUNDERSTOOD. BE SEEK ONLY TO GIVE WORDS TO THOSE WHO CANNOT SPEAK. TOO MANY WOMEN IN TOO MANY COUNTRIES. I SEEK ONLY TO FORGET THE SORROWS OF MY GRANDMOTHER'S SILENCE. THEY SAY IT IS DIFFERENT NOW (AFTER ALL, I AM ALWAYS VOCAL AND

confident

She poses before the "skinny" mirror on the back of her bedroom door. The mirror that gives her self-esteem a boost as it subtracts ten pounds from her fat clothes.

She test-drives her smiles. Quick and flirtatious. Heavy-lidded and mysterious. Wide-eyed and innocent. Slow and seductive.

Leaning in, she finger-flattens the part in her hair to inspect her roots. A touch-up, she wonders? She bares her teeth like a horse at auction. Maybe one of those new whitening toothpastes?

She steps back for a full-length inventory and frowns. She made friends with elastic waistbands years ago. She turns her backside toward the mirror, looks over her shoulder, and runs her hands over the full curve of her thighs. What about water aerobics? She pauses. She looks again, probing the mirror for flaws.

"Nah." She tosses her head. "I've got the bait. I just have to find my animal."

She gazes once more at her reflection, crinkles her nose, and growls. Let the hunt begin!

Carol McAdoo Rehme

I love myself when I am
laughing. And then again
when I am looking mean
and impressive

Zora Neale Hursto

Confidence
IS A
FASHION
STATEMENT
Wear it
LIKE A
ROLE
MODEL

McCALL'S
2677
Miss size B(12, 14, 16)

FRONT INTERFACING

aware

A wise woman realizes there are no mistakes in life. Every experience—pleasant or unpleasant, good or bad—occurs so that she can learn to love and accept herself, and others, unconditionally.

Trina Janson

REAL

"Don't put a title on me. I am many things. I am a girl practicing to be a woman. I am an athlete, a dancer, a reader, and a hunter. I am complicated sometimes and I love to laugh. Why do we need to have titles? To be labled? Can't we just simply be?"

Elizabeth (Bitsy) Rongen, age 17

complex

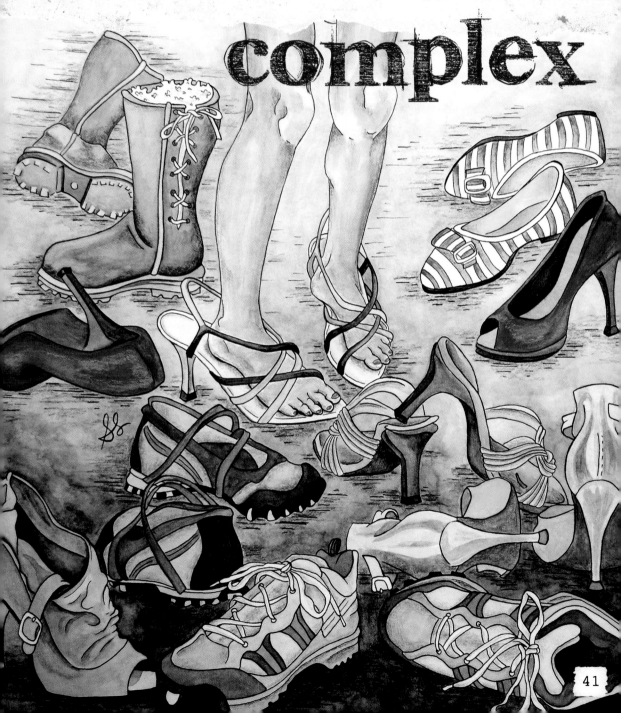

After I turned forty, I realized this hermit crab felt stifled and needed to find herself a new shell. I certainly had no regrets for dedicating myself to my family, maintaining our household, and taking a job that suited the life I'd created. But I'd always felt the sting of envy when I met people who were obviously passionate about their careers. I wanted what they had.

I felt I had something more to offer the world, another part of myself to give. I could no longer suppress my desire for a new adventure. The time had come to take myself, and my dream of writing, seriously. The mere thought enthused me and I wore a huge smile for days.

Doubting my success was simply not a consideration. My urge to pursue a new path was greater than any fear of failure.

Keep both feet on the ground, commanded the rational voice in my head. *Don't get any crazy ideas. Don't think you can actually earn money this way.* Yadayadayada.

Fortunately, I ignored that nagging dialog and allowed passion to rule. With the support of my family and a lot of courage, I knew, I just *knew* I could learn to write. I decided to make the leap.

I had offered my utmost to parent my four children, with no guarantees for success; now I crawled out of my shell to make the same investment in my new venture. I dared to find, and follow, my passion!

Jacoba de Boer-Wiersma

"Opportunity is like a hair on a bald-headed man; it only comes around once and you have to grab it while it's there."

Joycelyn Elders

SHE WAS FREE TO DREAM

gutsy

"Lo●sen your girdle and
let 'er fly!"
Babe Didrikson Zaharias

44

daring

She decided to start living the life she imagined.

I want to be the woman of your dreams. I want you to be proud of me. I want to be strong, positive, dedicated, and resilient. But I am also human and I guarantee I will let you down (and it will break my heart). Be patient with me, my love. I am not perfect and cannot be perfect.

Sometimes, I don't know how to express the feelings that scare me the most. I don't like to admit that I messed up. When I do decide to let you in, to confide in you, I am my most vulnerable.

Angela Harris

flawed

earthy

Giving unconditionally. Receiving unabashedly. Breathing relentlessly. Flowing incessantly. Pulsating feverishly. Mothering abundantly. Loving eternally.

Peggy Lee Hanson

fun-loving

"Old age ain't no place for sissies."

Bette Davis

By ninety-six years of age, Marie had outlived two husbands and both her children. But she still lived in her rural home—thanks to a crew of caregivers. Thanks to her friends.

Marie relied on them all. Each helper had an assignment. One brought the mail every day; another picked up her groceries. This one did her laundry; that one chauffeured her to the beauty shop. Someone else drove her to church and the rare doctor appointment.

But she had an especially close relationship with Jean. Almost half her age—and nearly half her size—petite Jean was a bubbling bundle of energy.

Jean brought over racy romance novels; Marie recited improper limericks. The two shared a feisty history of heart-to-heart confidences and irreverent jokes, touching stories and outlandish lies—and Christmas at Jean's for the past twenty years.

And it was Jean who was "sitting" with Marie that night after medication for an infection left her aged friend shaky, disoriented, and confused.

"I believe I'd like to soak in a bath," Marie suggested.

"Are you sure you feel up to it?" Jean worried that Marie was weaker than she thought.

But Marie insisted; so, after helping her elderly friend from bed to bathroom, Jean sat outside the door to keep her company and to give her privacy. After a time, she heard the water draining.

"Do you need some help, Marie?"

"No, I'll pop right out. You just wait."

She waited—and waited. "Marie?"

"I can't do it, Jean. I can't get out. My knees just won't work right."

Jean stood in the doorway to assess the situation. There sat Marie, folded in the bottom of the deep, claw-footed tub. Ancient, wrinkled, and … naked as a jaybird. Her once-buxom friend's solid frame had dwindled in recent years until she was nothing more than bones and lots of sagging skin, but still considerably larger than Jean.

"Uh, Marie, I think I'd better call the fire department. They've rescued other people in similar situations."

"No, you *won't* call the fire department." Marie was horrified. "I *know* those people. They're … men! Why, I'd be the talk of the entire community." She looked down at her accordioned body. "Besides, I need a good ironing."

They both began to laugh. Still grinning, Jean climbed into the high-sided tub, shoes and all.

She edged behind Marie, put her arms around the water-slick woman, and lifted. Up came a lot of loose, corrugated flesh. But Marie stayed put. Jean tried again. The same thing happened. Tears of hilarity weakened them both as she strained even harder. But only Marie's skin cooperated.

Exasperated, Marie finally ordered, "Jeannie, just throw my tits over the side and maybe the rest will follow!"

Marie leaned forward, Jean's adrenalin kicked in for one final heave—and they soon found themselves on dry ground. Giggling like girls, the two of them dried off, dressed for bed … and added a new story to their repertoire. A "steamy" one.

Carol McAdoo Rehme

49

stalwart

Daughter, mother, sister, friend
Dishes. Laundry. There is no end.
Chef, nurse, teacher, maid
Multitasking and underpaid.
Piano, soccer, and ballet
Same routine. Everyday.
Years fly by; no time to rest.
Children grow. Empty nest.
Grandma, wife, compassionate friend
Losing loved ones, trying to mend.
Devoted mother, gracious wife
Peace within. Fulfilled life.
Caretaker, companion, faith and religion
Generations of remarkable women.

JoAnne Hassen

sassy

"It's the
good girls
that keep the
diaries; the
bad girls
never have
the time."

Tallulah Bankhead

> "Don't try to make me grow up before my time..."
>
> Louisa May Alcott

naive

wishful
[wish-fuhl]

adjective
1. having or showing a wish;
desirous; longing.

Shouldn't age have
its privileges?

I always thought by the time
I was fifty, I'd have this
weight issue figured out,
crossed off my list. Now I'm
hoping for the next decade!

On a recent trip to the grocery
store, I was reminded that age
has no boundaries when it comes
to diets, a harsh realization and a
glimpse of truth.

**Lead me not into temptation.
I can find the way myself.**
Jane Seabrook

wishful

At the checkout counter, a sassy-looking octogenarian unloaded her cart. A size Junior Plenty, she filled the conveyer belt with V-8 juice, celery, carrots, apples, broccoli, two heads each of romaine and iceberg lettuce, bags of sugar-free candies, and six boxes of Slim Fast in flavors I didn't even know they made. The final item she tossed on was a hardcover edition of *The South Beach Diet*. Then she placed a rubber divider stick between her purchases and mine.

No worries, honey, I thought, *I don't even want what you're buying.*

As the perky, slender cashier rang up the produce, she assessed her customer from top to bottom. Meanwhile, I noticed how the elderly woman's eyes darted back and forth—from her stack of healthy choices to the temptation on display, a visual tug-of-war with her conscience.

Her eyes moved up and down the rack. Her fingers caressed a Twix, Almond Joy, Mounds, 100 Grand bar, Kit Kat, and finally hovered over a bag of M&M's. She looked at me. She looked at the svelte cashier. She looked at her cart contents. Hesitating, she moved to the end cap to drool over Fritos, Cheetos, and chips of every flavor. She eyed tabloids featuring the newest diet crazes.

"Your total is $191.71," interrupted the cashier.

The pleasantly plump customer hurriedly grabbed three Twix bars and a tabloid sporting a skinny, airbrushed woman in a skimpy bikini, and tossed them onto the counter.

"Is it too late to add these on?"

The thin, fit cashier shook her head in disapproval and growled, "It's fine."

"And can you put the candy bars in a separate bag so I can carry them with me?"

The skinny snip of a cashier slapped the sack onto the counter.

I completed my small transaction and followed the would-be dieter out the door, where I found her curbside, feverishly downing a Twix bar from her stash. As I walked by, she smiled. A piece of gooey chocolate dangled from one of her grey chin hairs.

She grabbed my arm, halting me mid-stride. "I hope you never have this problem." She sighed. "I've been dieting all my life and I seem to get nowhere."

Tight, blue-grey curls bounced as she tossed her head with a laugh and peeled back the remainder of the gold wrapper. "I think I shall start my diet tomorrow!"

indomitable

At fourteen:
The eldest of nine, I am a first-generation American. From parents and grandparents who migrated, Russia to China to Brazil to the U.S.A. We spend any and all extra time working the farm. Homework is a nuisance in my mom's eyes. So are programs and plays.

I am a freshman and beg to continue attending classes.

"No, they will teach you to smoke cigarettes at school," says my mom.

I promise to keep up with chores. Get an after-school job at Dairy Queen. Help our family with the money. It works.

At seventeen:
I have an opportunity to serve as volunteer coordinator at a domestic violence shelter. I try translating the word "volunteer" to a parent focused on feeding a large family.

"How much do they pay?"

I know when to say what. "Mom, it's good practice. Like training for a future job." That, she finally accepts.

In our conservative religious community, being single at my age is a disgrace.

"Did you find a husband yet?" Mom nags daily.

"I barely had my first kiss!"

"You'll go see relatives in Canada and Alaska." She means I'll look for a husband there.

I'm the oldest. I have to set an example.

But as for me, I will always have hope

At twenty-one:
The aunts nudge, as well. Weary of swimming against the tide for four years, I pick one. I marry. He is loud and wild, a party boy all the way, and—in the end—much like the men I counsel against at the shelter. He makes me quit working there.

At thirty-one:
I am done. Ten years of abuse is too long. A few near-death experiences. Enough. I have three daughters to consider.

Divorce is forbidden in my church. Anonymous letters find their way to my mailbox, condemning me for leaving my marriage.

I'm moving forward. Standing tall. Finding my own identity. What didn't kill me makes me stronger.

I seek Christian counseling, guidance from a yogic guru. I continue daily conversations with God.

Now:
My daughters are teenagers. Marital conflict is foreign to them. I thank God daily that I left my marriage when I did.

I read the words below an exit sign splashed across my daughter's art project: *There's always a way out.*

Marina Semerikov

57

mysterious

Don't say a word
Just let me feel you
The You with no name
Behind the action, the thought, the form.
Let me dance with this stillness
Drink your thirst
And savour your hunger
In this place with no night or day
No past, no present, no future.

I have no eyes to see
No ears to hear
No fingers to touch
I feel you with my heart that doesn't beat.
In this nothingness we are born and die
A tiny flame burning
And turned into a thousand stars.
That's where I found you
The you within you
And lose myself in this being.

Gloria Chan

After yet another crazy night—full of breastfeeding my eleven-month-old and cuddling the three-year-old who loves to sleep between my husband and I in the early hours, I wake to greet my five-year-old. I put a smile on my face and prepare breakfast, in spite of my deep desire for just five more minutes of sleep.

The day skitters by, full of cooking, dishes, cleaning, playing, dancing to a song with my daughters. Some tears. Lots of laughter. I submerge myself in thirty minutes of a mind-enlarging book while the girls nap. A text message arrives from my husband: *I love you and the effort you give to our family.*

At night, when the house is quiet and the candles are burning, I think back to my ordinary day, grateful for an amazing life that makes me feel so alive and important. Knowing my role in our family is vital. Understanding motherhood is priceless.

Astra Türk

content

This is the 1950s and my pride rests in the hands of boys who do the asking. I am waiting for a particular boy to ask me to dance, but the best junior high jitterbugger never does.

The most popular boy in school lives across the street. He is a basketball star, although he has not yet grown into a man's height, and is the best dancer in my neighborhood. He always dances with the girls who will kiss him.

I am not one of the girls who want him, but I like to watch the revolving door of his picks. And what I really love is to watch him dance. His impeccable rhythm and knowledge of the latest steps dazzle me.

One day I am twelve and the next I am sixty-three. The decades brought me the marriage of my dreams, three incredible careers, and a life in which I have been me. One of my greatest passions is dancing. My childhood girlfriend is coming into town for the fiftieth anniversary of our high school and talks me into going.

A small group of my classmates attend. One man walks up. "Elynne? Elynne?"

I struggle to remember his face. When he states his name and smiles, I recognize the star dancer of my adolescence, my former neighbor, the jock my pre-teen girlfriends lusted after.

We catch up on the moments that have brought us through six decades. As other classmates arrive, I greet them warmly. These are the people of my youth.

When the band begins playing our old tunes, I walk toward the dance floor and turn. He catches my eye as I motion him to join me. The best jitterbugger in sixth grade takes my hand and we meld into a graceful and wild ride, singing the words and matching our steps to each beat. He is still a great dancer.

When our dance ends, I motion to another classmate and then another. I had never danced with any of them when we were young. Now I am the one doing the asking. I choose and pick my partners.

I smile to myself. I will always love the girl who was twelve, the spectator, but a woman of sixty-three never felt better on the dance floor.

Elynne Chaplik-Aleskow

independent

60

K Osborne

intuitive

One bitter winter's day, I drove my son to his after-school daycare. Temperatures hovered near zero. Strong winds and blowing snow caused a dangerous wind chill of minus-seventeen degrees. While my son chatted about his day, a strong feeling compelled me to take a different route. As if on autopilot, I found myself turning the car onto the next street heading north.

"Why are we going this way?" my son asked.

"I don't know. Something's just telling me to drive this direction." I couldn't shrug off the prompting.

"Oh," he answered simply. "That's probably God tugging on your heart."

I reached for his hand and smiled.

Normally, the busy neighborhood bustled with cars, buses, and children, but today no one lingered outside; the area was quiet and empty. In the next block, a young boy and girl walked down the sidewalk, her head leaning hard into his shoulder, his hand gripping her bare fingers. The wind tugged at her skirt and icy snow pelted her pink tights. I knew the lightweight jackets they wore were scant protection.

The tug on my heart was stronger. "Those poor babies shouldn't be out here. Let's check on them."

As we drove closer, the children turned toward us and I gasped. The little girl wasn't wearing tights. Her bare legs were bright pink from the cold! Snow covered the front of her coat as if she'd fallen and tears streamed down her chapped red cheeks.

"I don't want to scare them," I said, thinking about the stranger-danger we enforce with our kids, "but I'd like to stop and help."

My son perked up. "I know that kid! He was in my second grade class. And I think his sister is in kindergarten."

That makes us practically not strangers, I reasoned as I pulled to the curb and opened my window. "Hey there. Is everything okay?"

My son leaned over to smile and wave at them. Recognition flickered in the boy's eyes and he gave a gusty sigh of relief. "We walked home from school, but we're locked out of our trailer." His voice shook. "I couldn't find the key we always hide outside."

The memory spurred his sister into another fit of tears.

"We're walking to my mom's work," he added with bravado.

"It's terribly cold outside. We'd be glad to drive you to her," I offered.

The kids climbed into the backseat. When I bundled the girl in my long coat, she turned shyly into her brother's side and peeked out at me.

"So, where does your mother work?"

"She works at McDonald's," the boy answered with pride.

I glanced at my son, whose face mirrored my realization: McDonald's was more than two miles away. And in this weather! "Then McDonald's it is. Off we go!"

In a few short minutes, we delivered the children to their mother and listened as—in one big breath—they told her about the locked door, the snowstorm, and how scared they were. The boy still clasped his sister as she smiled and waved good-bye to us.

Neither my son nor I will ever forget the prompting that urged me to follow a different course that day. God. Tugging on my heart.

Dawn Woods

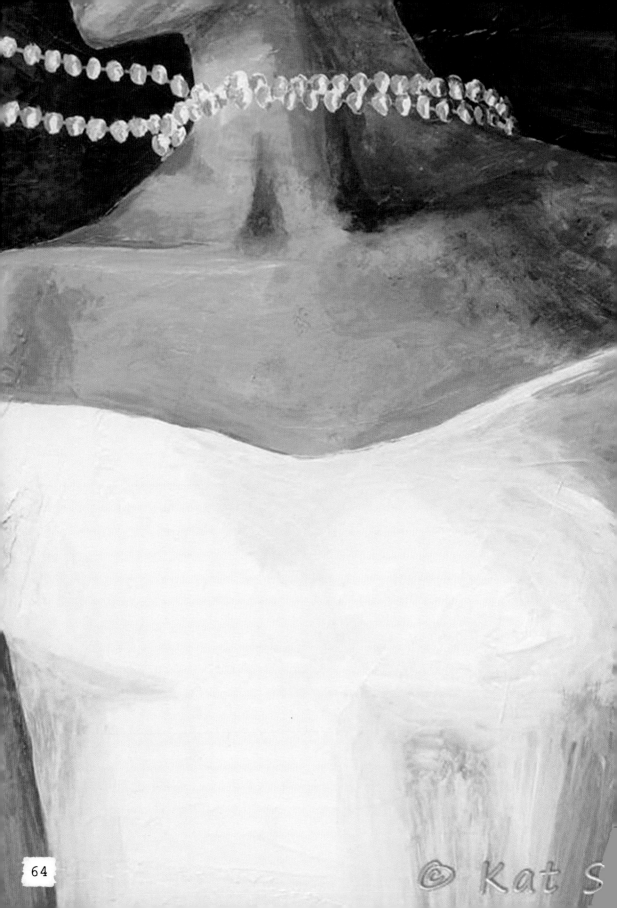

© Kat S

womanly

Flow ~ Femininity is a flexible, two-way flow; it is about giving and receiving in equal measure.

Emotion ~ Women are natural relationship builders; we use our ability to develop genuine bonds with the people around us. Our inherent competence to express vulnerability, compassion, and kindness enables us to connect.

Magic ~ Recalling the wonder of childhood brings playfulness to life. Don't take yourself too seriously. Recapture the magic of having fun. Just … be.

Inspiration ~ Our core strength lies in our aptitude for influencing others in a positive way.

Nurture ~ Not every woman is called to motherhood or flowerbeds. But all of us can support and encourage growth. In ourselves and others.

Intuition ~ Femininity is a blend of awareness, knowledge, and experience. gut instinct over rationalization, a connection to a higher cognizance, a subconscious impression that steers us in the right direction.

Natural ~ Femininity comes from the inside. It's not something that you put on or wear; it's your genuine, authentic self.

Energy ~ Feminine women are an absolute force of nature. A spark courses through us. From this, we derive our sense of inner strength, passion, and power and convert it to embrace and create a full life.

Claire Brummell

If she is lucky, there comes a time in a woman's life when the phrase "I have become my mother" is the greatest realization and compliment she gives herself.

Julie Rao Martin

mature

Women are like seashells,
colorful and dramatic, delicate
and subtle, each one glistening in
brilliant sunlight. Unique. Individual.
With a beauty all their own.

Brenda Elsagher

original

ten·der
[ten-der]

adjective, ten·der·er, ten·der·es
verb, adjective
1. soft or delicate in substance; not
hard or tough: a tender steak.
2. young or immature: children of
tender age.
3. delicate o
blue.

tender

Look at everything as though you were seeing it either for the first or last time. Then your time on earth will be filled with glory.
Betty Smith

I was what today would be labeled a strong-willed child. And I had an advanced case, because I haven't completely outgrown it. I knew how to push the hot buttons that would send my mom in a tailspin, and I loved the feeling of control. It was a game I won each time I drove her to the edge. Yet, no matter how I had acted during the day, every night she told me she loved me. Every night. How do you love someone who drives you nuts?

I thank God daily Mom lived long enough to see me have children of my own to temper my temperament. I've learned I need not orchestrate life as though others are puppets on a string. Now, when I tuck my three children (one very strong-willed) into bed, I, too, say, "I love you."

Easing her in, careful not to push or pull too hard, I positioned her on her handicapped chair inside the shower. Keeping her face out of the steady stream of water and yet wanting to keep her warm enough, I contorted myself like a Las Vegas Blue Man.

Freshly pressed and dressed, complete with makeup and hairdo, I found it awkward to keep dry while bathing my sixty-nine-year-old mother.

Singing "Amazing Grace," I gently wiped the sweat beading her brow and moved my way down with the washcloth in a systematic approach. Time, I noted, was not on our side. Mom would weaken from the sheer exhaustion of following instructions, even from me lifting her limbs.

"I'm going to wash under your arms now and turn you just a little so I can get your back. Is that all right?"

"Uh huh," she mumbled.

Oh my goodness, I realized, *this is the first time I have ever seen my mom naked.*

Disease and a recent stem cell transplant had taken their toll on a pretty, physically fit, pep-stepping woman lovingly known as Golfing Granny. Now she was frail. Fragile. Vulnerable.

Hearing her moan with fatigue, I knew I needed to hurry.

"Scoot over, Mom," I said. Taking the plunge, I stepped into the shower, clothes and all. Fully drenched, hair stringing, with eyeliner dripping down my cheeks, I knew there was no turning back. Not that I would. This was my gift; this was what I could do for her in that moment.

At my feet, I noticed a puddle of black mascara swirl like so much dirt sucked down the drain. *How fitting,* I thought. Cleansing water flowed as gently over our bodies as a brook during spring thaw, softening harsh memories and healing our past. The experience bonded us without words.

In the sweetness of the moment, Mom cupped my face in her hands, meeting me eye-to eye, woman-to-woman. Mustering her strength, her words barely audible, she spoke. "Honey, I don't think I have ever seen you more beautiful than you are right now."

Our tears mingled in the mist. Once again, I felt her unconditional love, her forgiveness, her acceptance. Already, I was grieving the mother of my childhood.

indulgent

When I was a child, we called Sunday "Gramma Days." Grandpa and Uncle Jack were there, too, but Grandmas *was* the day. She made it hers, from the bowl of red-Jello-with-bananas to the weekly cache of penny rolls.

Her busy hands must have prepared for us hours ahead of time—homemade potato salad always waiting, jelly jars standing with spoon handles sticking out of them. Summers meant freshly squeezed lemonade and flat pans of ice cracked into chunks in the *zink*. In winter there would be sweet tea with milk and a sugar sandwich to fold and dunk.

Her fingers were old and arthritic when I first saw them; still, she faithfully sifted through the buckets of cherries Grandpa brought in. She cut shortening into flour, pressing the mixture in her fist to explain the evolution of piecrust to a small girl. She signed her flaky pastries with leaf-shaped signatures from which cherry steam escaped as we waited for them to cool.

At the end of the day, she handed out packets of pennies wrapped in aluminum foil. As precious as real silver, each roll had been molded by her hand, ripples resembling the finger waves she pressed into her hair each morning. Fifty pennies each. No more, no less. As she placed them in our eager hands, her eyes narrowed with laughter. I could imagine her going through her fruitcake tins of change and searching the hidden corners of her purse, fingers darkening from the grimy coins.

A blue-flowered bib apron is all that remains now of Gramma Days. But she is there still, as I fasten the apron around my waist, crimp a piecrust with the tines of a fork, and wrap copper with silver for eager little hands.

Debra R. Borys

adventurous

I've stayed in the front yard all my life. I want a peek at the back where it's rough and untended and hungry weeds grow.

Gwendolyn Brooks

"Be courageous. It's one of the only places left uncrowded."

Anita Roddick

unfinished

One of my college professors once pointed to me in a classroom of my peers and announced that I would be saying something important in the future. I was so proud at that moment. This man, this teacher, could see into my soul and tell that I was somehow intuitive, or gifted, with something special to say that the world wanted… no, *needed* to hear.

It seems strange that, so many years down the road from that shining moment, I can't imagine what he was thinking. If I had something to say, surely I'd have found sufficient time to say it by now. Yet I am awkwardly silent.

Maybe I did have something to say. Then. Somehow I lost the path that led to my inner self. The one that helped me decide who to marry and what I believed in, or not. I wonder why I just drift like others seem to, following the drone of their lives, day after day, not worrying past this month's bills or this year's promotion.

If I still have something to say, why don't I say it? It occurs to me that maybe I have said something already, just by living, just by being. In that, I might take some comfort. If. If only I knew. If only I could see in myself what he thought he saw in me.

Kitty Sutton

© Kat Shoa

I was only forty-two and in the space of a few hours I had become a widow.

Most people think the earliest days are the hardest, but that isn't true. There is too much to do during that time. First I had to comfort our two teenage children. Then I had to make phone calls to let people know what had happened: My husband, three months short of his fiftieth birthday, had a massive heart attack and he didn't linger … was only part of the story I repeated numbly.

Everyone was shocked. Arrangements had to be made. Friends and family offered comfort and help. The wake and funeral were well attended; he was a well-liked man. I cried myself to sleep at night but during the day I rarely shed a tear. The cemetery service was the most difficult, as I watched the casket being lowered into the earth. Then suddenly everyone was gone, leaving behind more food than we could possibly eat, and the same heartfelt offer: "Call if we can do anything."

What could anyone possibly do? Already, I knew the doing was up to me. Somehow I had to go on, to put my love behind me, and ignore the pain in my heart. It was much easier said than done.

My children went back to school. Although I had two weeks bereavement leave from work, I couldn't stand being home so I went back after a week. The first day was difficult. Co-workers and partners and other attorneys in the law firm came by my desk to offer their sympathy, even though most had been to the funeral.

Each day on my way to and from work, I passed Lake Washington, and as the months wore on the deep water drew me. My pain was so great and I thought how much easier it would be to just drive over the grassy bank and
into the water. No more pain.
No more sorrow.

durable

One day after work, I pulled onto the grass, parked, and just stared at the water for a very long time. I put the car in drive. But when I started to press my foot on the gas pedal, I was confronted with images that refused to go away. My son. My daughter. My elderly parents. What was I thinking? How could I do this to them? How could I do this to myself?

A state trooper pulled beside my car. "Are you all right?" he asked.

I started to cry, pouring out my anguish to this total stranger.

"Go home," he urged. "Call a friend to come stay with you. Get through tonight and tomorrow go get help."

He followed me and waited until I was in my house before he left. I phoned my best friend Gert, who arrived within half an hour, and we sat talking half the night at the kitchen table. In the morning, she contacted a psychotherapist who lived not far from my home. He gave me an appointment that day and I spent two hours with him.

It was a long road, but I got through it. I took those first painful steps. I changed the bed linens, letting go of my husband's scent. I donated his clothes to the Salvation Army. I packed a box of mementos I couldn't part with, including love letters and a book of Rudyard Kipling poems in which my husband had inscribed: *To my beloved Nancy.* Never again did I consider suicide, but I had come so close. Today I'm almost seventy-four. I've lived a good life and been married and widowed two more times. People tell me I'm a survivor, but I prefer to think I found an inner strength I didn't know I had.

Nancy Clark Townsend

When life is at its worst, you become your best. A sprinkle of grace overcomes your heartache and allows you to change, to find your purpose and passion. You choose to live the God-given Gift of Greatness that unlocks the fullness of life.

Melanie Brown

adaptable

Never bend your head. Always hold it high. Look the world straight in the eye.

Helen Keller

Life isn't always fair or easy. Your reactions to it shape your life.

In November of 1983, my father died. My mother was thirty-nine and had four children, one of whom was mentally disabled. Mom had no job, no high school diploma, and no life insurance policy on my father. She fell into a depression for a time, but snapped out of it. She knew she had to do something so she could care for her children.

In the spring of 1984, she received her GED and we "graduated" together. That fall she started college with me. Only eighteen, I was horrified at the thought of going to school with my mother. But I soon realized what a strong woman she was and I was proud to walk the same halls with her and even share a class. Five years later, she graduated and became a licensed social worker and landed a job in our hometown.

Now I realize just how amazing she really is. A quote hangs on her wall that sums her philosophy: *Life isn't about waiting for the storm to pass; it's about learning to dance in the rain.*

Mom has weathered many storms, but she's learned to dance through them.

Sherry Nelson

Blessed is the season which engages the whole world in a conspiracy of love.
-Hamilton Wright Mabie

steadfast

When my husband and I moved back to our hometown, we both groaned a little, wondering if we'd made the right decision. Years later, still in the same house on the same street, we sit on the patio at night thanking God for bringing us home.

When we first arrived, I met eight new women at a welcome party. We bonded. We had coffee together almost every day. We kept each other sane. We helped when the kids were sick and we worried when someone looked too tired, too thin, too anxious. We taught each other how to cook and how to give home permanents. We heaped praises on the smallest of achievements. We talked about God and we prayed together and we held each other when we cried. We relied on each other's strength.

And we called ourselves The Birthday Club.

In 1968, I gave birth to twins, a boy and a girl. Both were born with congenital hip defects. Hospitals and surgeries became part of our lives. When he was a bit older, my son required open-heart surgery, in an era when open-heart surgery was barely practiced.

We arrived at the Mayo Clinic just before Thanksgiving one year, prepared for a lengthy six-week stay. By then, I was pregnant with our sixth child.

When our weak little boy was released from the hospital at last, I was anxious to gather the four children we'd farmed out for the past month and a half. Christmas, I realized to my horror, was a mere two days away and I hadn't given it a thought. I was too exhausted, too drained to contemplate the holiday ahead. I simply wanted to be home.

My eyes widened as we drove up to the house. We were welcomed by an open driveway cleared of snow. By a fragrant tree twinkling in the living room. And by gaily wrapped gifts standing at attention beneath its branches. In the kitchen, I discovered a refrigerator bulging with food, the holiday turkey, and seasonal treats. Without a doubt, I knew where to place the credit, who to thank for salvaging our Christmas.

That New Year's Eve, a healthy, beautiful baby girl came into our lives.

And back they came, eight women running to help me heal, to clean my house, and to feed my family. Friends, tireless friends, at hand to make me laugh again.

Forty-five years later, The Birthday Club regularly convenes. Even in our vintage years, the original eight of us still share clothes, sip wine, and put our arms around each other. We praise kids and grandkids, and we might even share an occasional recipe— but we don't perm our hair anymore!

Collette Conati

Miss Katzor taught speech and debate in 1955. She stood at the back of the room, gesturing and swooping with encouragement as I stumbled through my first contest at age sixteen. When I saw her, my confidence returned and our team got first prize.

Frankie Finch—music, dance, and exercise consultant—appeared at General Mills in 1970 wearing a pencil skirt and spectator pumps. "You hold such promise," she said. "I see such good in you." Her words carried me onward for more than three decades. She left me with the gift of confidence.

An escapee from Poland, he appeared at the National Speakers Association in 2008. He called a week later, wanting to get to know me. I said I was busy. He called again. I said I was sick. "Then I will come out and help you," he said. I opened the door and my life changed. Gratitude blew in, my enthusiasm for life ramped up—and the gifts of Frankie and Miss Katzor became mine to give.

Mentorship is a boomerang gift. Words flow out—then come back, ready to be given again.

And, in case you need to say them or hear them, the words are:

"You hold such promise."

"Let's do it!"

"Let me help you."

"I see so much good in you."

"Your life makes a difference."

Janie Jasin

moody bloom

The experiences girls face in high school are endless: from making the right friends to causing the least drama to getting a spot on a varsity team. And parents wonder why we like being alone in our rooms for hours on end!

Mariah Christian, age 18

intentional
[in-ten-shuh-nl]

adjective,
1. done with intention or on purpose; intended: an intentional insult.
2. of or pertaining to intention or purpose.

Ten years after working in corporate America all over the world, I settled into a new marriage and a new job in the heartland of America, North Dakota. An aerospace company created a position for me in upper management, where no woman had ever gone before. I was definitely paving new paths in a male-dominated arena. Okay, paving would be an understatement.

> Be bold. If you're going to make an error, make a doozy, and don't be afraid to hit the ball.
> Billie Jean King

The first day, I ransacked my closet, wondering what to wear. The corporate blue power suit? Or the black one? A pair of slacks with a nice blouse and understated-but-distinguished scarf?

I chose a suit.

Hoping I looked enough the part to gain some credibility, I walked into the Monday morning meeting with my male colleagues. Truth be known, I wasn't even sure what the hell they were talking about and, apparently, my suit and my bluffing skills weren't convincing anyone.

About fifteen minutes into the meeting with these thirteen gentlemen, one looked at me and lifted his empty mug. I waited to confirm what I couldn't believe. He tilted it slightly from side to side to show it was empty; his glance swept across the coffee pot—and back to me. I hadn't misinterpreted his meaning.

Not that I have anything against serving coffee, but to expect it in that moment seemed odd. I decided my reaction to his non-verbal request would set an unshakeable precedent. Could I maintain a corporate demeanor and earn the respect of these men at the same time?

It was evident that the others around the conference table were uncomfortably aware of the silent scene unfolding. Deciding to set a firm boundary, I leaned toward the gentleman and quietly said, "Ah, don't you just hate it when your legs break like that?"

Muffled laughter came from most of the other men, who seemed to admire my moxie. When I left the boardroom that morning, I wanted to shout, "Forget the glass ceiling. I just blew the windows out of the Empire State Building!"

Looking back now, I realize how much I loved my job and all the men I was privileged to work with. They taught me about airplanes and I taught them about working side by side.

RWR

How many friends do you have? Not parents (although mine have been with me through thick and thin and they always will be) or family members. I'm talking real, true friends. Friends you would trust with a secret they would take to the grave? Friends that have your back and would do anything for you?

I have four. Four. I look at it as quality, not quantity.

I know a lot of people. I have a lot of Facebook "friends" and I run into acquaintances most everywhere I go. But true friends are hard to find.

My closest friends grew up with me in a small town. Even though geography separates us now, it never matters how much time goes by; we always pick up right where we left off. I can call them (and sometimes do) anytime, day or night. If I need them, they come. We have seen each other through it all: growing pains, marriage, kids, divorce, jobs, breakups, depression, death, roadblocks, sickness, and surgeries. They hop on planes and drive through blizzards to be with me, listen to my doubts, and set me straight. They put things in perspective. The older I get, the more I appreciate having these people in my life. Someone once said that good friends are like stars. You don't always see them, but you know they are there.

Michelle Turnberg

appreciative

animated

"I am still determined to be cheerful and happy, in whatever situation I may be; for I have also learned from experience that the greater part of our happiness or misery depends upon our dispositions, and not upon our circumstances."

Martha Washington

She picked idly at the loose button on her favorite blouse and stared at it without blinking. She should get out a needle and thread and tighten it, she supposed, but it simply took too much effort.

Nights like this were the worst. Once the kids were bedded down, the empty evening stretched endlessly before her. Not that there wasn't stuff to do—like this button. With a growing family, there was more than two people could get done.

But that was the problem. There weren't two. There was only one.

At first she'd tried to pretend he was still deployed. She and the little ones were used to his tours of duty and everything it entailed: sending care packages, taking turns during the occasional phone calls, emailing pictures. A quick press of the Send Button, and their grinning faces would appear somewhere in Iraq.

A dry sob erupted from her chest. *Did Joe see it? Did he have time to check his email that morning before …*

They said the blast that killed Joe came from another crazy suicide bomber. How could someone think so little of his own life that he was willing to sacrifice it for the sole purpose of taking the lives of others?

Her other. Her other half. Her Joe.

She gave a fierce tug at the loose button and watched it fall into her hand. *It didn't make sense.*

But then, nothing made sense lately. Even this place. Fort Drum wasn't much different than any other army base and she was used to finding friends wherever the whim of the military sent them. Only this time she wasn't yet settled when Joe was deployed. They'd spent every precious last minute together as a family, right up to the moment they waved goodbye when he boarded the plane.

The bombing occurred only a few days after he arrived in the Middle East.

No miles of any measurement can separate your SOUL from mine. -muir

Everything happened so quickly. Not that it stopped women from showing up when they heard the news. Military wives cared for their own, finding strength in sisterhood. They arrived promptly at her doorstep. With casseroles. And offers to help. Two even volunteered to dispose of Joe's clothes.

The clothes he'll never need again. The thought was a bullet piercing the emotional dam she'd erected and her tears gushed through the hole.

She pressed a pillow to her mouth to muffle the wails she could no longer contain.

Joe, Joe, I miss you so much. I want you back. I want you home. The kids need you. I need you. She felt hollow and so alone. *I want your arms around me, holding me.*

When her sobs waned to an occasional hiccup, she drifted into an exhausted sleep on the overstuffed couch. But a soft, persistent rapping at the front door roused her.

Someone's here? She glanced at her wristwatch. *At nine o'clock?*

She smoothed her hair and unlocked the door. "Yes?" She recognized the faces but didn't know their names.

"We're sorry to come by so late." The two women on the stoop eyed her puffy face. "But—we have something for you and felt an urgency to deliver it tonight."

"For me? Come in."

The women placed a soft mound on the dining room table. "Suzy and Krista brought us your husband's clothes and …"

Suzy? Krista? Then she connected the names to the ones who'd packed up and disposed of Joe's personal things.

"… we're members of Going to Pieces, the quilting guild here at Fort Drum." They smiled. "We—all of us—made this for you."

They spread the bundle on the table and smoothed its folds.

"From Joe's clothes?" Her eyes widened in wonder at the quilt. "You made this from his clothes?" She traced a block with a trembling finger. Pieces of desert-sand camouflage, fatigues, dress uniforms.

The women nodded. "Every piece came from your husband's slacks and shirts. The pattern we chose is Lover's Knot. It seemed— symbolic." They lifted the quilt and wrapped it around her shoulders.

She snuggled an edge to her cheek and closed her eyes. "It's like Joe's arms," she whispered. "Like he's here, holding me again."

When she finally looked up, the women were gone.

I didn't thank them and I don't even know their names. She frowned in consternation.

Her brow cleared. It didn't matter. She knew who they were. She had recognized them by the goodness shining from their eyes and the empathy spilling from their hearts.

Carol McAdoo Rehme

When every woman goes within,
nurtures her true self and lives her
passion, the whole world shifts.

Tonya Sheridan

balanced

As a little girl, I spent part of each summer in South Dakota with my grandparents. When my grandfather, who was a U.S. senator, died, Gram finished out his term. She was one of the first women to serve in the Senate. I remember her not for her service to her state and her country, but for the love she showed her grandchildren:

Scraps of old nighties sewed into doll clothes.
Snapdragons speaking in Gram's silly voices.
Stories and songs shared on the porch swing.
Sparklers and sprinklers.
Cakes made of sand.
Fresh lemonade served in tall glasses.
Solitaire, sugar cookies, lavender soap.
Falling asleep in the room by her attic.
Lulled by night noises, secure with Gram near.

Ellen Javernick

radiant

you are beautiful

discerning

My sister is my identical twin.

However, when I look at her, I see more than the physical traits that mimic mine. I see her talents as she sings, writes, and organizes. I see her knowledge as she graduates with a master's degree and helps children become better readers. I see her strength as she and her family endure the flooding of their home. I see her wisdom as she raises teenage daughters. I see her grief over the loss of our parents. I see her joy as our family circle continues to grow. I see her loving and caring ways as she reaches out to others.

Most of all, I see the mirror image of the One who created us all and loved us into being.

Janel Kresl

the *Creative Mind* plays with objects it Loves

Inventive

Sometimes
I am a crazy woman
    who sleeps in her clothes
        under a mound of quilts
the house brilliant with lights, doors unlocked, the oven still on.

If I were older,
        and not by much
my children would worry
            whisper about my forgetfulness
            note my decline into eccentricity
they would exchange knowing looks, eyebrows raised
and shake their heads.

They only see the finish
            spent like an empty cartridge
            glistening in the grass.
They don't hear the fire and flare as the bullet of words
        shoots through my mind and out my fingers
        splattering on the page,
            a glut of words littered like collateral damage.
They don't witness the triage of words into
        good and true, nice and right.

I get up, turn off the lights and oven
        peel off days-old clothes and bathe.
Sipping fresh coffee, I celebrate
the birth
of one more poem.

Bonnie M. Benson   95

spiritual

When Jo entered, the whole room lit up. At twenty-five, she was a beautiful, bubbly young lady whose eyes twinkled with mischief and joy. She was a wife, mother, daughter, and teacher. When she left us, the world went dark.

Among the memories of those first days is the physical weight of my heart. It felt heavy. It literally hurt. Each time I looked at my son Jamie and his twenty-two-month-old daughter, I could only question, *Why?*

My husband dealt with Jo's death in his own way. "If only," he kept saying.
If only Jo had taken the good car, the windows would have been cleaner.
If only she had left the house later.
If only the sun hadn't glared in her eyes.

But my son spoke only of his wife's strong faith. How he and Jo had talked about death. How she knew her God and wasn't afraid to die.

Jo inherited her strong beliefs from her mother. Roberta had modeled unfailing faith; through the earlier loss of yet another daughter and through the death of a husband, Roberta had found her strength in prayer.

She had first-hand experience with the anguish our Jamie was experiencing. She understood that—although the heartache never goes away—life continues and good things come out of moving on and living to the fullest. Even in the face of Jo's fatal car accident, this indomitable woman prayed for Jamie's future, selflessly hoping our son would cherish Jo's memory while forging a new life, a life overflowing with love and a replacement mother for his young daughter Jacy.

I, too, have found healing through prayer as God replaced the ache of death with tender memories of the past. Years later, I am inspired by Roberta as she's enlarged her prayers to include Jamie's second wife and their sons.

And I am reminded of Jo's legacy of faith each time I say bedtime prayers with my granddaughter and her little brothers. They always repeat the prayer that Jo once taught Jacy:

> Jesus Savior wash away
> All that has gone wrong today.
> Help me every day to be
> Good and gentle, more like thee. Amen.

Jody Hauge

She kept the

faith

All the other women her age wore fussy dresses, but not Grandma. She was the first in her neighborhood to wear pants suits. She never went back to skirts. She was confident in her own sense of style, and a key part was her red plaid jacket.

Made of wool in a swing style, it was cream and gray and red, with over-sized buttons and big turned-back cuffs. Since she never learned to drive, Grandma walked all around town wearing it, looking hip in slacks and turtleneck, very Katherine Hepburn-esque. Grandma is long gone now, but I still have my memories. And her plaid jacket.

Betsy A. Riley

chic

Can you imagine a world without men?

No crime & lots of fat happy women.

audacious

valuable

I think we are realizing that the relationships we have with our girlfriends are as important as the career, as important as the marriage. They are sovereign.

Rebecca Wells

> "No matter where you go or what you do, you live your entire life within the confines of your head."
>
> Terry Josephson

pensive

staunch

The oven timer went off. Although she could hardly tolerate eating them, breaded fish sticks had become a regular entree in her ever-developing portfolio of meal plans. He could digest fish better than most anything else, so she would fix it for him, and together they would dine.

Finding palatable food was one small skirmish in a larger war. His cancer was back and she refused to allow the insidious disease—or the necessary chemotherapy—to zap the life out of him. Through trial and error, she was discovering foods he could swallow with less reflux, less gagging. No, she would not allow cancer to easily claim her husband. She would persist, through prayer and patience, to preserve the rich and simple life they had built in their fifty years together.

She spent her energy frugally during the weeks when nourishing meals went mostly uneaten, when daily phone calls with faraway family took time and attention, when routine housework expanded to include his chores, as well as her own. She used her scant reserves on frequent trips to clinics, pharmacies, and grocery stores. Everyday tasks cost her more in physical, mental, and emotional energy than they had before his cancer returned. But she always found a measure of replenishment on his good days, days when they could take a car ride into the countryside to gain a minute sense of normalcy.

Two years later, the two of them sip coffee in the sunroom he had added to their snow-bird home the previous winter. Twelve months chemotherapy-free. Clear blood tests. No sign of the tumors.

"God is good," they say to each other.

"God is good," this woman of resolution says to herself.

Brenda Finkenbinder

"Without a test, you have no testimony."

Unknown

LOVE is ?

In the early morning hours, well before dawn, my boot-clad dad clomps in, urging me to get up. It's hunting season! I tug on my long johns and orange outer clothing. While Dad tosses back his third cup of strong cowboy coffee, I sip the hot chocolate he prepared to warm me for the sub-zero weather.

I make my way to my deer stand, exhilaration pounding through my veins and, with a firm grip, pull myself soundlessly up the primitive ladder. Perched at the top, I absorb the early morning sounds. Leaves crackle, small animals squeal, and deer grunt. I can hear my own heart pound. Senses heightened, I wait for dawn. Careful not to move, I canvas the woods, searching out a trophy buck.

After two hours of unsuccessful posting, I climb down to join my uncles and guy cousins at camp. We warm ourselves at the wood-burning stove in the primitive house built by my great-great-grandfather, an immigrant from Norway. We tell the same stories every year. We cook camp food on old stoves and manage without running water and use the original outhouse. Most girls squirm and grimace at the thought of it; but me, I think hunting rocks!

Elizabeth (Bitsy) Rongen, age 17

unconventional

grateful

To appreciate the joys and crosses God allows in our lives is truly a blessing. Each day is filled with opportunities to serve others, to suffer for the greater good, to celebrate new accomplishments, to love and enjoy family and friends. Yet, how many wish only for the joy, love, and celebrations? I admit I do not ask for the pain, heartache, and suffering; yet, in the deepest recesses of my heart, I understand God knows what I truly need. He provides the "opportunities" that allow me to grow and bloom into the woman He intended me to be. I am learning to be thankful for *all* the circumstances in my life.

Arlene Johnson

nurturing

When I gave birth to our second child, he was born with a cleft palate. There was a hole in the roof of his mouth and his newborn cry sounded like a foghorn. In spite of the milk teeming at my breast, my baby was unable to eat; he had to be fed with a tube inserted into his tiny nose. The doctor would surgically graft the tender linings of my infant's cheeks to build a soft palate and uvula. Meanwhile, the woman who shared my hospital room delivered a baby who needed breast milk to survive, but she was unable to nurse her child.

I fed her hungry baby at my aching breast and my new friend gathered me in her grateful arms.

Collette Conati

HOPE

S

If the Shoe fits

buy it.

impulsive

Truth

Paradi

complicated

LOVE

109

prepared

I was planning my mother's funeral and chatting on the phone to Julie, one of my best friends.

"You'll need lots and lots of food," she said.

"Why?"

"Well, you're the host family."

I love to throw a good party, but really, the *host family*? We weren't Jewish. We weren't going to be sitting Shiva.

"And wine and beer," she added. "Lots of wine. You have a big family and they like to sit around and laugh and talk. Yes, you will need lots of wine and beer. I know these people. And get some gin and tonic. Limes too. "

Julie knew what she was doing. Both her parents had died years earlier. She was a pro. Me? I'd never thrown an after-party for a funeral before. I think you only get one shot when it's your mother. And my mother in particular would be mortified if I couldn't throw a good party for her. She was, after all, referred to as "the belle of the ball." I had to get working.

Thing is, I've never been good at providing a lot of food. I come up short. Always. Once my siblings and their spouses and children start arriving, it's hectic. Like the circus, but with more of a freak-show feel.

The night before everyone was to arrive, Julie called. "Got all the food?"

"I'm changing the sheets on the beds and getting the house ready. Do you think this is a Holiday Inn?"

"No, I think it's the Ritz. But the restaurant is closed, and the guests are in nice rooms. And very hungry." Snark. Snark.

> Women can make sure that as long as we are leaning on each other, we are also protecting and celebrating one another.

Sonja D. Curry-Johnson

"Shut the hell up," I said with love. We have been friends since second grade. Julie had been there through my life's changes: my breasts blooming like perky pansies in ninth grade; my breasts dropping like pendulous peonies at menopause.

She knew me. She was trying to help. She was also getting on my nerves.

The next day my family arrived. From 8:45 a.m. until 5:36 p.m. people were shuttled to my house from the airport. They arrived hungry.

At 6:15 p.m. Julie pulled up in a van. She slid the side door open to heave out a red wagon. She loaded it with coolers and pulled it behind her like a volunteer for Meals-on-Wheels at her first stop.

"You look like hell," she greeted me.

"I feel like hell." We laughed, and she pushed me to the side by my shoulder. "Get out of my way so I can get this food in."

"What food?"

"Oh, *please*." She rolled her eyes, hauling her wagon to the kitchen.

Julie took out dozens of Tupperware containers, all color-coded (the telltale mark of a third grade teacher). She had coolers with lasagna, a hot dish, brownies, and cakes. All homemade.

"See these people?" She tilted her head toward my family and friends—
"Think of them as army ants. Visualize a tethered cow smothered in ants, asphyxiated and bleeding internally from the insects swarming in through its ears, mouth, and nose. They can strip a chicken in a day."

I gagged, but it was a great visual.

"Thank you. Thank you," I said as I hugged her.

"That's what friends are for." Then she wheeled her wagon to the van, came back in the house, and helped us celebrate my mother's life.

Molly Cox

envious
[en-vee-uhs]

adjective,
1. full of, feeling, or expressing
envy: envious of a person's
success; an envious attack.

I think women can be each
other's toughest critics. We
want what other women have:
beauty, homes, possessions,
husbands, money. We'd swap
our children for theirs, if
it were legal. Like so many
others, I have focused on
outward appearances—and been
jolted by wake-up calls and
swift kicks-in-the-ass that
refocused my priorities and
emphasized my blessings.

She strutted the mall like a model on the runway. Long blond hair—with natural waves. Magazine-perfect makeup—with shimmering blush to accent her high cheekbones. An adorably short skirt, crisp white blouse—and chic two-inch pumps.

Of course she would wear heels. Who doesn't push a stroller through the mall wearing two-inch dress shoes?

Even her carriage was stylin', a newfangled, high-end contraption that did everything but change the baby's diaper. Cup holders held her drinks, a soy latte in one, a designer water bottle in the other.

I contemplated ducking into the bookstore to hide behind — I mean, browse a large display. I shoved my second-hand stroller through the doorway.

"Reneé, is that you?" she squealed. She ran up and threw her arms around me. "Reneé Rongen, I haven't seen you in years. It's me, Olivia! I hope you remember me."

Really. Could anyone forget Olivia?

She was captain of our high school cheerleading squad, an accomplished ballet dancer, and the girl boys mooned over. Teacher's pet, she always went the extra mile to make sure she was the center of the world, flirting with everyone in her path.

No, I hadn't forgot Olivia. Truth be told, I was glad to leave her in the dust when I walked out of high school.

She paused near my stroller. "Is this your little boy? He is adorable."

I leaned in to brush the cracker crumbs from his jeans and tee shirt and swipe at the orange juice ring orbiting his mouth. While I was there, I tried to smooth his unruly hair. He tugged at the swanky gadgets on Olivia's stroller and grabbed the fancy toy from her daughter's tray—to taunt her baby with it.

And what a baby.

Couldn't she be ugly? With snot running down her nose? Lunch staining her pristine pink tights and frilly pink dress?

The baby flashed me a pageant-ready smile.

While Olivia detailed her shining life, I tried to ignore my second-oldest pair of Levis topped by a wrinkled tee complete with splattered ketchup, a lunchtime battle scar. My glance slid down, settling on my ragged, high-top Converses.

Why today? Why not yesterday, when I was dressed up and wore makeup? My hands slid to tighten my ponytail.

"Let's stroll around and visit and have a cup of coffee," suggested Olivia.

Don't waste time on jealousy. Sometimes you're ahead, sometimes you're behind.

Mary Schmich

Gnawing off my left foot appeals more. "I'd love to!" I gushed, in spite of myself.

We wandered the storefronts, reminiscing about the good old days. *Really were they so good?* At the coffee shop, I insisted on paying. I suppose I wanted her to see I could afford not one, but two cups of coffee, and espressos at that. Our conversation waned.

"Are you happy?" I asked. *What? Where did that come from?*

A smiling Olivia began a long, seemingly rehearsed, answer. But somewhere in the middle, she dissolved into tears. "No, I'm not happy at all. I'm getting a divorce."

I handed her a tissue and listened to the brow-raising story of her husband's long-term affair. *But she and Mark were the Barbie and Ken of our school.*

Remembering the good-looking quarterback that made our knees knock when he walked near our lockers, I wanted to pound her husband and yell, "You've got the whole package, you idiot. And you ruined it!"

Instead, I recalled the girl who only dreamed of becoming a wife and mother. And was Olivia happy today? Hell no! I found myself comforting my distraught classmate.

At the end of our chance meeting, we exchanged phone numbers—and we used them.

Over the years we grew closer. Our roles reversed. She wore Converse tennis shoes at her job in a manufacturing plant. I became the cheerleader on the sidelines, rooting for her, encouraging her, and building her self-esteem.

Today, Olivia is living her dream, head-over-heels with her average-looking second husband and the adorable stepsons she gets to mother. Olivia is happy at last … and my Converses fit better than ever!

RWR

I wear my cape around my waist

multi-tasking

Inside every woman is a special blend of strength and sensitivity. She dons her Wonder Woman cape over her business suit, high heels sticking in the mud at her child's soccer game, while her toddler rests on her hip and spits up on her silk blouse. She clutches a briefcase under her arm and presses a cell phone to her ear, arranging meetings, comforting a friend who is going through a tough time, checking on her elderly parents, searching out her teenager's whereabouts, reassuring her spouse delayed on his flight … which leaves her solely responsible for yet another twenty-four hours.

She can handle it. She will stretch her physical and emotional capabilities to the limit and beyond. She will oversee homework, cook dinner, do dishes, pack lunches, give baths, read bedtime stories, make fundraising plans for a local charity, feed the dog, and type a report due the next day at work.

She will make cupcakes for the school bake sale, gather outgrown clothes for the church service drive, sort piles of laundry, take out the garbage, pay the stack of bills, unclog a toilet. She will ignore the head cold she caught from her toddler—and the untimely cramps, bloating, and moodiness coming on because …

… she has bigger problems. Her teenager finally staggers in, late for curfew, and vomits the first alcohol he's ever consumed and needs comfort and hugs and a serious heart-to-heart discussion.

Tomorrow is nearly here and the cycle will begin again. Carpools, dentist appointments, groceries, commutes to the city, board meeting presentations, music lessons, vacuuming, a stop at the dry cleaner, school projects, dinner, dishes, baths and bedtime— and a late-night rendezvous with an amorous spouse.

And she will do it all because that's who she is. That's what she does.

Nancy Runstedler

fragmented

Daughter, mother, sister, nurse, wife, friend,
mentor, educator, student, caregiver.
What strength it takes to fulfill these roles.
Overwhelmed sometimes, I scream silently
inside rather than show my hurt and pain.
I stand tall, because I know so many are
depending on me. And I embrace this gift,
finding my strength in God.

Cynthia J. Hickman

enthusiastic

I have a friend whose age adds up to more years than mine. But she maintains her zeal for life and looks for the positive in every situation. Years have taught her that life is short, share it and enjoy every moment. She does.

At the ring of the bell, her door is flung open, the coffee put on, and the table set. Her ears are always tuned to hear, and she has the best laugh in the world. Her motto? *If it ain't fun, we don't do it.*

Connie Nelson

sensible

I scratched with my fingernail at the spelling words I'd penciled, but they glared back at me, racing willfully uphill instead of marching obediently along the ruled line the way I'd been instructed. I rubbed the paper with my finger and, having a bit of luck, wet my thumb with the tip of my tongue, and pressed harder. But the lead only smeared, darker and uglier. Tears welled in my eyes at the sight of the ragged smudge on the crisp page of my spanking new Big Chief tablet. I rubbed again.

Miss Townsley's plump hand stilled mine. "Carol," she leaned down to whisper, "that's what erasers are for."

"But now I've ruined it."

"Mistakes aren't worth crying about."

Kneeling beside my desk, my first grade teacher reached for the gum eraser in my pencil box and demonstrated. With a few flicks of her wrist, the spot disappeared.

"See? Now you can start fresh and try again." She smiled and tousled my penny-red hair. "That's what erasers are for."

Even today, those words calm my spirit and ease my mind. When I'm faced with rewriting an awkward passage or reworking a chapter that stalls the storyline, I think back on Miss Townsley's wise counsel. And, with a few flicks of my wrist, I delete in complete agreement and start fresh.

That *is* what erasers are for.

Carol McAdoo Rehme

stern

One November morning I woke up late for school, which would not have been a huge deal, except—I am the teacher. Suffering a major hangover from the previous night's drinking binge, I called in sick. I sat on the edge of my bed, stared at my pathetic reflection in the mirror, and started to cry. My life was so totally out of control; something had to change. I knew it and I knew that my best friend knew it as well. I picked up the phone.

Lisa, who lived two hours away, didn't hesitate. She promised to drive right over and take me to a treatment center to get the help I needed. While I waited, I downed a few beers and had a change of heart.

"I'll be fine," I insisted when she arrived. "I don't have a problem and I don't need any help."

Thankfully, Lisa was honest and loving enough to point out the pain and harm my drinking had caused. Not just in my life, but in the lives of those around me. Our discussion intensified. I argued. She persuaded. Ultimately, she convinced me to climb into her van. But I drank beer the whole trip, knowing that it would likely be my last.

Although I was humbled and remorseful those first couple of days at the treatment center, I soon wanted to leave. I called Lisa and begged her to drive me home.

"You need to stay, Sherry." Love laced the firmness in her voice. "They'll give you the help you so desperately need."

I stayed. I've been sober since that cold November day in 2004 and I couldn't have done it without Lisa. She has been my best friend, my biggest cheerleader, and a huge support to me. I am truly a better person for having her in my life.

Sherry Nelson

123

When Brenda, a full-time working mom, wants to combat the bitter North Dakota weather, she makes a huge pot of spicy chili. And she doubles the recipe.

Her mouth-watering meal feeds the multitudes—a bowl for an elderly friend, a large batch for the newest residents across town, a container for a family of six.

"Stop at the house and grab the blue to-go carton from the garage refrigerator," she whispers and winks. Drawn to her sweet-as-sugar smile, people do as she asks; they take the path to the friendliest fridge in town.

Using her mouth-watering concoctions, Brenda empathizes and sympathizes. Her food whispers courage to those in trial, welcome to those new to the neighborhood, goodbye to those moving.

Through the years, countless numbers have visited her garage. Most of the small town has eaten from her pantry. Quietly, she goes about her business, finding more ways and more recipes to make her community happier—one dish at a time.

Katie Dilse

nourishing

stubborn

A.W 3·11 83

"I refuse to think of them as
chin hairs. I think of them as
stray eyebrows."

Janette Barber

awesome

amazing

Y
O

present
[prez-uhnt]

adjective,
1. being, existing, or occurring at this time or now; current: the present ruler.
2. at this time: ~~at hand; immediate: articles~~

True to the adage, the older I get the more I realize how much I don't know. What I do know is: As I age, moments are sweeter, times together are more valued, and times apart seem to last longer. I've always operated my life from a master checklist, immediately tackling the next great adventure, but a recent birthday and a new commitment to myself have me reveling in the present. My bucket list for the next half-century is not about crossing off places I've been or mountains I've climbed, but rather to feel all that I can in the moments where I am.

> "You must learn to be still in the midst of activity and to be vibrantly alive in repose."
>
> Indira Ghandi

"Mom, what do you want for your birthday next week?" asked thirteen-year-old Grace, my younger daughter.

Of course, I responded like any woman about to celebrate the twentieth anniversary of her thirtieth birthday. "Oh, honey, I don't want a thing other than to spend it with you and the rest of the family. I just wish for a restful and peaceful day. That is what I want."

"Come on, Mom! This is a really big birthday. What do you really, really want?"

"A peaceful, restful day," I repeated.

At 5:30, the morning of my monumental birthday, I was treated to breakfast-in-bed with all the trimmings. I sat up when I heard a tuneful chorus of "Happy Birthday" and found a smile from somewhere, trying to appear alert and alive. My husband Tom bore a tray of burnt toast, burnt egg, an assortment of juices, and a cup of coffee with real cream. Grace held something behind her back.

"I got you exactly what you wanted for your birthday, Mom. And the best part is I didn't even have to spend money on a card! Isn't that cool?"

Tom smirked, but before I could respond, Grace offered her gift—a beautiful red rose enveloped in sprigs of baby's breath and fresh greens. A deep burgundy ribbon printed in gold calligraphy draped the vase.

"Isn't it perfect?" Grace blurted. "It's exactly what you wanted!"

I fingered the ribbon and nibbled my lip to keep from laughing as I read the sentiment. *Mother, Rest in Peace,* it said.

RWR

trusting

Being the best pregnant mom I could be, I had my routine prenatal check-ups done on time and with good humor. I waited, warm jelly on my bulging tummy, for the ultrasound technician to say, "Looks good and on track." But she hesitated.

She called the doctor in and they went over things again. My husband and I held our breaths, wondering what they saw.

"Markers," we were told. "There are markers for Down's syndrome. Combining your age with the markers, you have a chance of giving birth to a baby with Down's." She let that news sit with us for a moment, then continued, "We can do an amnio test to get a positive result, if you would like."

She mentioned that a lot of women opt to terminate pregnancy under these conditions. But my husband and I agreed it wasn't even an option—this was our baby, no matter what.

A week later, I stood on an overlook, the mist of Iguassu Falls washing over my face, small rainbows dancing around the cascades. I shut my eyes, feeling the moist air on my body, and prayed. For my baby, my family, and me.

It will be okay. It will be okay. It will be okay. God spoke directly to me and I heard him.

Back again at the doctor's office, I had another ultrasound. The markers had disappeared! I smiled and knew that must be what God meant. I gave birth to a beautiful daughter with long blond hair—and Down's syndrome.

And it is okay.

Ann Martinka

reflective

After the death of her mother, my sister-in-law Joyce began the arduous process of cleaning out her mother's home. Her mother was not the warm, sweet kind of person people were drawn to. At most family functions, she wore a sour look and sat by herself, smoking one cigarette after another. When she did speak, her comments were negative. Was it any wonder I always wanted to avoid her?

One day, Joyce appeared at our doorstep, toting a huge box filled with rocks and seashells her mother had collected from her travels around the world. Most were in little bags labeled with the location where each had been found. Neither my husband nor I took an interest in them.

Months later, the dusty box resurfaced in the garage during our annual spring-cleaning spree. I felt guilty that neither of us had placed much importance on the keepsakes. *Might as well clean them, too,* I thought, and carried them to the kitchen sink.

The yellowed labels held surprises. One identified pebbles picked on a walk to the Holy Church of Nazareth, another stones from Syria. I discovered an array of shells from the Red Sea, Fuji, Australia, and Florida, each carefully chosen through the years to evoke a memory.

Who knew the memories would be *mine?*

I picked up the bags and read more labels. The Bahamas. The Caribbean. The Mediterranean. Ah, I could feel the balmy breezes and smell the salty air. I closed my eyes and imagined Joyce's mother—not as the crusty loner of her later years, but as a giggling young woman. An image flashed: laughing over her shoulder at her new husband as, hair streaming, she ran along the beach. Perhaps they went back to their room, made love all afternoon, and talked into the starry night.

I remembered she'd been a young widow, left with four small children. How she must have grieved! What a blessing to find joy again in a second husband who enjoyed traveling and wanted to show her the world, a world full of new promise.

My fingers picked pieces of colorful coral from the box, some battered and broken from the passage of years. I thought of Joyce's mother, widowed a second time. Her deep grief, her declining health, her lack of interest in the outside world—the same woman who had so painstakingly labeled each stone, each shell she'd collected with such devotion.

And then I stumbled upon it, in the very bottom of the box. A rock from the Wailing Wall. *David picked up rocks like this to use against Goliath,* read her note.

My hands stilled. *What was the Goliath in her life?* I wondered. *Widowhood? Pain? Loneliness?*

Suddenly, the dusty box of mementoes took on new meaning and I knew I would never look at women the same way again. No more judging, I decided. From now on, I would peer beneath the surface, search out the surprises, and dig to the bottom to discover the true woman hidden there.

Brenda Elsagher

I had a friend that I was very close to in high school. When she went off to college in another state, she changed her name. Oh, not legally. She had a name like Elizabeth, with a variety of shortened versions such as Liz, Betsy, Eliza, or Beth. So my friend picked one, kind of like selecting a flavor of ice cream. I was stunned. In that moment, I learned that a woman might redefine herself from one day to the next. She can decide who she is and who she wants to become.

Lisa McLeod-Lofquist

decisive

fashionable

LOVE

is patient

LOVE

is kind

it does not envy

it does not boast

it is not proud

it is not rude

is not self seeking

it is not easily angered

keeps no record of wrongs

LOVE

does not delight in e

But rejoices with the TR

It always PROTECT

always trusts,

Always

hopes,

always perseveres

LOVE

never fails

1 Corinthians 13:4

reverent

From an early age, I was fascinated by my grandma's wrinkled face. Her skin looked like soft dough that had been pressed by a triangular screen, creating lots of tiny, three-sided pillows. Her cheeks were as puckered as a quilted cloth. Grandma was never vain, but she was always neat in appearance. She'd just swipe a bit of powder across her nose "so it doesn't shine" and maybe dab some rouge on her cheeks, if it was a special occasion. She kept her hair short, in a finger-wave style that reminded me of flappers in the twenties. She always used dusting powder—Cashmere Bouquet. I like to think each wrinkle was a result of the life experiences she wore so well. I hope mine develop as lovely as hers.

Betsy A. Riley

DON'T *Strive* for PERFECT but rather AUTHENTIC

Shoving the vacuum into its home in the hall closet, I stifled a groan. A half-day of housework behind me and I still wasn't ready for the out-of-state company expected any minute. My four small children whirled through, leaving a wake of toys, crumbs, and stray shoes scattered across the recently trackless carpet.

And then I saw it: the sliding doors of the family room. The ones I had washed and scrubbed earlier that morning. Generous finger streaks and tiny nose prints daubed the freshly polished glass panes.

"And that looks like ...." Frowning, I stepped nearer and bent for a closer inspection. "Why, it is! Peanut butter and Oreo cookies smudged all over. Those kids!"

Near tears, I plopped onto the couch and grabbed the jangling phone.

"Hello?" I growled.

"Hello, dear," answered my mother from her own couch a state away. "Are you busy?"

"Oh, you have no idea! We're expecting guests and I just can't seem to get all the housework caught up around here and the kids...."

"That reminds me," she interrupted. "I should do some of my own. Housework, that is. The mirror above the couch is smeared. But, you know, every time I look at the sweet baby prints your little ones left there last month, I can't bring myself to wipe them away. After all, I'm still showing it off to my friends as 'priceless artwork!'"

My gaze ping-ponged around the room. A half-eaten cracker here, wadded socks there, tilting towers of picture books in the corner. And four tracks of footprints framing it all. I grinned.

Crowning everything was a hand-painted masterpiece on the patio doors. Un-numbered. One-of-a-kind.

My own piece of priceless artwork.

Carol McAdoo Rehme

carefree

On June 17, 2004, I lost by best friend, my husband, my soul mate. Phil's death left me empty. Sad. Searching for a way to go on.

One rainy day, I left the house on an errand for the first time without Phil. At the store, I noticed a shiny penny in the entry. My husband used to send me roses: singly, by the dozen, even splurging for fifty of them to mark my fiftieth birthday. Now, seeing the coin, I realized there would be no more fragrant bouquets. I stooped and picked it up—it was like a sign from Phil—and returned to my car in tears.

As the days went on, other pennies appeared.

On a trip with my daughter to Alaska (a place Phil and I had planned to visit), I discovered a penny. During a three-mile cancer walk in Florida, I noticed one more on a spotless street—no litter, no leaves, just a single shiny penny. While filling the car with gas one blustery, sub-zero morning, I was indulging in a pity party when I picked up yet another.

I mentioned to a friend at lunch one day that I hadn't found a penny for a while. When we left the restaurant, *three* were lying on the ground. I think Phil was making up for lost time!

I keep the pennies in a jar. At last count, they totaled fifty-six, the number of years we were married. Each coin I find is a reminder from Phil to carry on. Life is good. Happiness is wherever I choose to find it.

Kay Miller

sentimental

love

"To get joy we must give it, and to keep joy, we must scatter it."

John Templeton

trailblazing

Modern woman is mother, friend, lover, professional, caregiver, problem solver, entertainer, economist, crisis prevention technologist—and much more. Her life roles are unique to this generation, and she doesn't have a manual to follow. Yet she succeeds in today's world with determination to be the person she is meant to be.

She falls down but picks herself up and keeps going. She loves, lives, solves problems, and starts over as many times as she must. She protects those close to her. She provides for them. She takes time for herself so she can be her best for others.

She faces many choices and discovers that her journey takes unexpected detours. She overcomes her obstacles and builds character and knowledge. She lives and leads by example—and she's not afraid to share her story. To encourage a new generation of women rising to face a challenging world.

Janice N. Richards

exacting

I tentatively approached the glorious Victorian home of an accomplished, candid editor willing to evaluate my book.

"Hello?" I called through the screen door.

"Hi, come in here to my office." Wearing funky glasses that belied her seventy years, Judy Delton sat behind a large desk. A jeweled cane leaned against a walker nearby.

We didn't waste time on chitchat; this woman charged by the page for her expertise.

"Hand over your manuscript," she said. "Hmm, I'm going to read the last page too."

I gulped. "Will that cost me another $150?"

"No," she laughed. After reading it, she asked, "Did you say you were a hairstylist? Have you ever written anything before?"

I shook my head and explained that colorectal cancer had made me rethink my life goals. "It took me until I was forty-two to realize I loved to write."

"This sample is actually pretty good. But you need to paint scenes with your words. Show, don't tell." She glanced up. "I want you to join my advanced writer's group as soon as you can."

"How much will that cost?"

"My, you are concerned about money. How about this? I like those gold bangles you're wearing. After I teach you about writing, you can give me a bracelet."

At the Sunday group classes, I learned that Judy—short, wide, with respiratory and joint conditions—was agoraphobic, had not left her home in two years … and was brutally honest about writing.

Reviewing my critiqued manuscript, I asked, "Is there a different meaning in the squiggles and the lines going across these pages?"

She laughed heartily. "No. They both mean the same. Delete those pages. In your memoir, you've written nothing but good things about your husband. No one is that kind. Make him real or take him out. And it's gagging with God. You also need some humor. It's too much for the reader to take in."

"You want me to find something funny about colorectal cancer?"

"God forbid you torture the reader this long. Yes, lighten it up."

My husband watched me delete marked passages and remove entire pages. He started referring to my project as The Booklet. I rewrote almost the entire book and had to agree it was much stronger Judy's way.

One day after class, I hung around. "Uh, Judy, I bought something for you." It's hard to purchase clothing for someone else, but the suede dress had simply insisted, *Buy me for Judy*. I hadn't been able to leave the shop without it. Judy was excited and teary and warmly accepted it.

I arrived home to a ringing phone. "It fits! And I love it!"

When he learned what I'd done, my husband insisted on calling her back. "Yes, yes. Glad you like it," he told her. "I have just one question. How many dresses do I have to buy to get my good image back in the book?" Judy snorted and they bonded.

The next week after class, I styled her hair. Gray-headed, Judy requested a chic cut and color—burgundy with splashes of blue, yellow, and magenta. Some might call her eccentric. I thought she was a creative genius kind enough to share more about writing every time we met together.

The day came when she handed back the remainder of my manuscript and I handed over a gold bangle. "It's funny and poignant, Brenda, just like you. I like the hint of God and a truer picture of your husband. Good job. Keep coming to my class. You can pay with a haircut once in a while."

Judy hosted a party and she told everyone about my husband and the dress. She died six short months after I met her, yet she changed my life forever. I keep her photo on my desk and think of her often. She pushed me to excel.

I still hear her voice in my head. "You can do better. Write more, write often, just write!"

Brenda Elsagher

candid
[kan-did

adjective,
1. frank; outspoken; open and
a candid critic.
2. free from reservation, disgui
subterfuge; straightforward: a candid
opinion.
3.
4

Beauty certainly is in the eyes of the beholder. It seems like only yesterday my daughters—now teenagers at seventeen and fourteen—were small girls splashing in the bath. At those times, we shared some of our best visits. If I ever wondered who I was in their eyes, the answer was revealed during those tender, open ... excruciatingly truthful ... moments.

" When something that honest is said, it usually needs a few minutes of silence to dissipate. "

Pamela Ribon

When Bitsy and Grace were five and three, they sat in the soaking tub of our master bath while I showered across from them in my neo-angle shower with the glass surround. Encircled by naked Barbie dolls and an occasional Ken, they made up stories as they bathed. I disrobed and scooted past the large mirror to dart into the shower. Let's just say I never had the body of the Barbies that surfed the waves in the tub.

I loved this part of my day, giggling to myself under a cascade of warm water as I listened to the jabbering of the precious girls we'd adopted. Occasionally, Bitsy asked me to clear a spot of steam from the shower door so she could talk to me face-to-face. I obliged, blowing a kiss through the small circle as I bent to shave my legs.

"Mom, I can't see you now. Make another spot," Bitsy demanded.
Doubled over, with gravity tugging my mid-section, I cleared away more steam and continued to shave.

"Mom, did you nurse me with those breasts?" Bitsy asked conversationally.

Proud that she used the proper term, but reluctant to offer more information than appropriate for their ages, I opted for a simple answer. "As a matter of fact, I didn't."

"Um, did my birth mom nurse me with her breasts?"

Clearly, I was not prepared to have this talk while the two of them eyed me, naked and exposed. "No." My response was quick. "No, she didn't."

Razor held just above my ankle, I paused, wondering how Bitsy would react. When no reply came, I sighed in relief, grateful to avoid a Big Topic in my vulnerable position. Poised to shave my other leg, I heard Bitsy say, "Too bad you didn't nurse me with your breasts, Mom. You have really good milkers. Long and pointy. They almost touch your belly button."

"Yeah, good milkers," Grace parroted.

I gazed down at myself, imagining things from their point of view—and nearly cut my leg.

"Uh, Mom?" Bitsy asked. "Can you clear off another spot?"

I pretended not to hear. "Oh, look," I said, offering a feeble distraction. "Barbie and Ken sure are cute going over those waves!"

RWR

> *Death leaves a heartache no one can heal;*
> *Love leaves a memory no one can steal.*
>
> Unknown

Cancer was eating away my daughter and I was mad at God. Yet I accompanied Kari to almost all her chemo sessions. She wanted someone with her to make sure she got the "right mixture."

"One good thing about this cancer, Mom," she proclaimed, "is that we get to spend quality time together."

After each treatment, we went to McDonald's for a fish sandwich and fries, the only thing that tasted good to her. We talked and shared many things in those short months. But the day she asked me if I thought her brother Kyle would sing at her funeral, I realized it was time to admit she was losing her battle, inch by inch.

In a choked voice I replied, "Well, you'll just have to ask him."

We lost Kari to colon cancer a scant year after the initial diagnosis. Kyle sang at her funeral.

I still think about my daughter every day. Last week I had a vivid dream. I was fretting about Christmas and all the preparations and how I would never be ready and suddenly I felt movement at my side.

I woke and saw my Kari. She was as big as life, and in life she *was* big. Her presence commanded attention and her laughter drew people together. Now here she was sitting on my bed.

"Mom, just shape up and get things in order!" she commanded. I had to blink twice to realize that it was just a dream. But I drew strength from my daughter that day and I'm ready for Christmas.

Judy Roelofs

devoted

daughter
you are
a true
original

emancipated

The longer you wait for a man to heal your wounds of rejection, the more time you waste. Instead, be adventurous and fruitful. Find your passion for life.

Mariah Christian, age 18

spirited

Soulful, fluid and ever-changing
Protective of those we care for
Intuitive and enlightened
Respectful and resilient
Tenacious and trustworthy

Optimistic by nature
Futuristic, fortunate, and friendly

Adorable and admirable

Warriors for humanity
Orchestrators improving life
Molders of meaningful relationships
Adverturers and explorers
Nurturers of faith, hope, and love

Lori LaBey

SPIRIT OF A WOMAN

"Even though we've changed and we're all finding our own place in the world, we all know that when the tears fall or the smile spreads across our face, we'll come to each other because no matter where this crazy world takes us, nothing will ever change so much to the point where we're not all still friends."

Unknown

loyal

Women suffer the pain of puberty, miscarriage, childbirth, infidelity, menopause, harassment, rape, pay inequity, sleep deprivation, heartbreak, wars, and death. Yet even in our darkest hours, when we have sunk to our knees in despair, we dig deep into the well of our souls and rise again to carry on.

Nancy Runstedler

undefeated

eAThe in

layered

"Women are meant to be loved,
not to be understood."

Oscar Wilde

challenged

Time with God is endless. What's hard is finding endless time.

Mariah Christian, Age 18

yielding

while it might seem like i have the most perfect life ever, which i mostly think i do, it is not without its many flaws. i am beyond fortunate to be in a position that i don't have to hold down a real job. in fact if i had a to have a real job, i don't think i would even attempt to try to do what i do. the frustration level would be more than i could possibly handle, however, my time is not my own. true, there are not

it's all about compromise

any physical time restrictions or schedules placed upon me, they still exist. they are self-imposed to a certain degree, but there are many, many responsibilities that i carry on my shoulders. not all my time can be spent creating my work. in fact very little time is spent doing that. it is a constant juggling act between family obligations and the demands of my work. a huge compromise at all times. often i feel i compromise the integrity of both, as it is a constant struggle to do what i feel is right. its hard to justify what appears to be doodling or scribbling in preparation for a project or workshop for days on end, when laundry is piled to the ceiling and the house is a wreck. proper preparation is paramount to my work and planning out workshops.

" Learn the wisdom of compromise,
for it is better to bend a little
than to break. "

Jane Wells

fulfilled

find your happy place every day

Women often wonder, "How do I know if I am on the right track?" The answer is simple. If you are being true to yourself, you are on the right track.

Tonya Sheridan

> "It isn't what I do, but how I do it. It isn't what I say, but how I say it, and how I look when I do it and say it."
>
> Mae West

spicy

Sexy. A word that packs more punch per syllable than all other words in the English language. It's yummy to say—and delightful to feel.

It's the purr of a woman during an intimate kiss and the luminous shine of her freshly washed hair. As she ages, taut skin and a perfect memory grow obsolete; wit, wisdom, and warmth take over.

Confidence. Playfulness. Power. You know when a woman has it. She drips it like a vanilla-bean ice cream cone on a hot Louisiana day. Sexy comes in all shapes and sizes, colors and languages. No parameters. No boundaries.

While I find it hard to narrow down the definition to exact components, I know what it is *not:* Valley talk; humor impairment; nasty, spider-veined, pasty white legs that haven't seen the sun since the Nixon administration. (My legs, for instance.)

To be, to feel sexy, we must tap into our divine feminine energy. And, if we're lucky, we can do it without squishing ourselves into Spanx!

Molly Cox

who are the women of The Birthday Club?

The nine women who called themselves The Birthday Club began as a social group in the rural community of Crookston, Minnesota—and grew to be so much more. But in the eyes of their kids they were known, often with a roll of our eyes, simply as Club.

"Mom's on the phone with Club."

"Mom is out at a play with Club."

"Mom's busy. Club. Again."

The ladies of The Birthday Club were my safe harbors. As a child, I ran to them and buried my face in their laps when I couldn't tell my own mom about feelings too close to home, about fears of inadequacy, about boyfriends she wouldn't approve.

I prayed not to bump into these women when I stayed out too late or went to places I shouldn't have been. I knew they would rat on me! They ratted on all the sons and daughters of their members, claiming it was for our own good. They held a common bond, truly all for one and one for all of the kids of Club.

My mom has shared her life with these eight women for nearly fifty years. They comprise an unlikely group, becoming stalwart friends as they shared rants and recipes, faith and fashion tips (or not), tragedies and triumphs. They wore tightly curled wiglets, marched their families to the front pews of church, and made dessert bars for PTA events. They were, in a sense, my second moms.

As I have aged past my fifth decade of life, I view these women as a collective source of wisdom. Through my own life experiences, I've witnessed the hardships they hoped to shield me from and the lessons they tried to instill.

To each of you—Gretchen, Judy, Pam, Collette, Connie, Kay, Carol, Gladys, and my mom Sharon, thank you for disciplining me, loving and listening to me, and always supporting and believing in me. You have been such inspirations in my life, epitomizing the true Spirit of a Woman.

I love you all!

RWR

accolades!!

First and foremost, I am so grateful for my husband Tom, who was my faithful cheerleader, and my biggest distraction, during the writing and compiling of *Fundamentally Female*™. He knew just when it was time for walking, boating, or tossing a fishing line in the water. I also want to acknowledge our children, Alexander, Elizabeth and Grace, for their patience and gifts of time, which allowed me to finish and meet deadlines.

I am thankful for my many girlfriends who have shared their triumphs and tears. Their life experiences created the "aha moment" I needed to realize that we as women are more alike than we are different. I recognized that we are cloaked in different clothes, different masks, but each of us yearn to be validated. And we all hope to make a difference in the world.

To those I have lost to death, I offer my bittersweet appreciation for participating in their life journeys. Each time I spread my wings, I feel them nudge me out of the nest. They opened my eyes to the present moment and awakened my soul to not only dream, but to grab on to those dreams and soar. Their deaths inspired me to really, really live!

There are no accidents, and so it goes that I found Carol McAdoo Rehme, the best editor in the whole world. I could never have finished this book without her giving me assignments and taking me in as her own. She stretched me, laughed with me, and was tough when she needed to be tough. I am thankful for the Divine Appointment of meeting her and having the privilege to work with her. It was an honor and one of the greatest learning experiences of my life.

I'll miss my late evening phone calls with my talented graphic designer, Annette Wood. From the get-go, out of all the artists I interviewed, she got the concept. Her enthusiasm and outstanding creativity continue to awe me. I'm so thankful she generously shared her gifts with me.

Dana Widman—whose photography is peppered throughout these pages—has worked with me for years. Her pictures always capture the moment. Perfectly. I appreciate her extra patience and willingness to go the extra mile during the late nights!

And who couldn't adore the authors and artists whose uniqueness is expressed within the covers of this book? They dared to be candid. They exposed their vulnerability. They generously offered their stories and art to the world. Their enthusiasm and excitement for this project and its progress amazed me. They kept me moving forward with their kind emails and the ultimate question, "When is the book coming out?"

Finally, I want to express my gratitude to you, my reading audience. Thank you for purchasing *Fundamentally Female*™ for yourselves and as gifts for others. Without you, there would be no need to print this book. I humbly hope the words and artwork resonate and stir within you the certain knowledge that you are never alone. How can you be, when you are surrounded by women who share your passions, your joys, your embarrassing quirks … the very traits that assure us we're *all* fundamentally female!

RWR

grazie   you're the BOMB

thanks!   kudos!

couldn't   merci
have done it   did I say
without you   thank you?

I'm so grateful
You ROCK

contributors

Maureen J. Andrade is a writer, artist, and mother from the Pacific Northwest. She publishes fiction and poetry at Fictionique.com and essays at Opensalon.com. She also teaches painting at the nonprofit Gallery 360 in Vancouver, Washington.

Bonnie M. Benson loves words and the things she can make with them: poems, plays, stories, and novels. In between, she wields needles, paddles kayaks, and swims long distances. Now she is exploring the Gulf Coast of Texas.

Jacoba de Boer-Wiersma, born and raised in the Netherlands, used her master's degree in business administration as a business consultant. Mother of two and stepmother of two, she is dedicated to her beautiful family. Jacoba works at the University of Minnesota, Crookston and has enjoyed writing since childhood.

Former Chicagoan **Debra R. Borys** is the author of suspense novel *Painted Black*. A freelance writer who spent eight years volunteering with the homeless on the streets of Chicago and Seattle, Debra is working on a second book in the Jo Sullivan series, about throwaway youth striving to survive.

Melanie Brown is well known for her contagious smile and enthusiasm. As a motivational speaker, she empowers people to step out of their comfort zones to live with significance. A John Maxwell Certified Speaker and Coach, Melanie knows the power of adding value to people's lives.
www.inspirationforournation.com

Through Feminine 1st, **Claire Brummell** helps women across the globe recognize the power in embracing their feminine core. She teaches women to rediscover and reconnect with what is really important to them. Claire gives women the tools to live the lifestyles they truly desire.
www.feminine1st.com

Leah Burke lives in Fertile, Minnesota, with her husband Todd and children Kiah, Carter, and Tyra. For the past twenty years, she taught English to junior and senior high school students. Leah appreciates the amazingly strong women in her circle of family and friends.

Gloria Chan was born in China, raised in Hong Kong, and spent thirteen years in Oxford, England, before relocating to the United States in 2009. She has two Pay It Forward acupuncture clinics, in Asheville and Hendersonville, North Carolina, and is the founder of the Asheville Pay It Forward Network.

Elynne Chaplik-Aleskow is a Pushcart Prize-nominated author and award-winning educator and broadcaster. Founding general manager of WYCC-TV/PBS and Distinguished Professor Emeritus of Wright College in Chicago, Elynne has performed in NYC and Chicago. Her stories and essays have been published in numerous anthologies and magazines.
www.LookAroundMe.blogspot.com

contributors

A senior in high school, **Mariah Joy Christian** is a three-sport athlete and captain. She plans to attend college, majoring in athletic training and massage therapy. Mariah loves to write and hopes to compile a book of her original and inspiring quotes.

Kim Clements and her husband have pastored in Sacramento, Concord, Phoenix, and Carlsbad. She taught junior high language arts for twenty-five years. The mother of sons Mychal and Taylor, she loves the power of a great story.

Collette M. Conati, a distinguished and refined seventy-five-year-old, lives a Christ-centered existence with her husband. They delight in their six children and their spouses, and their fifteen grandchildren. A campus minister, she uses her life experiences as a guide to help others through her church and community.

Molly Cox is co-author of *Improvise This! How to Think on Your Feet so You Don't Fall on Your Face* and producer of the award-winning film for caregivers, "Note to Self." A master of improv and sketch comedy, she speaks nationally about humor, self-care, perspective, and life balance.
www.mollyspeaks.com

Raising four sons in one of the nation's least-densely-populated counties is a task **Katie Dilse** doesn't take lightly. She's courageous. She's determined. She's quick-witted. Katie laughs, teases, and embraces life as a mom, keynote speaker, and community volunteer. Her electrifying personality and can-do attitude are unforgettable and extremely loveable!

Brenda Elsagher is a comic, international speaker, magazine writer, and author of four books: *If the Battle is Over, Why Am I Still in Uniform?; I'd like to Buy a Bowel, Please! Bedpan Banter;* and *It's in the Bag; and Under the Covers.* She also writes a blog and a humor column.
www.livingandlaughing.com

Brenda Finkenbinder resides in downtown Seattle, Washington, and on Long Lake near Bemidji, Minnesota. A small-business owner with her husband Michael, Brenda consults school districts and non-profits in administration, project development, and fundraising. She serves as Associate Teaching Director for Community Bible Study, Seattle.

Shari L. Fruechte developed her passion for life into a mission of helping others unleash the beauty that exists deep inside. A runner, she completed her first triathlon at age forty-three and her first half-marathon at forty-four. She will soon be a black belt in tae kwon do. Shari's personal life motto is: "Enjoy it all!"

Andrea H. Gold is president and founder of Gold Stars Speakers Bureau in Tucson, Arizona, and co-author of *The Business of Successful Speaking: Proven Secrets to Becoming a Million Dollar Speaker.* Andrea, a life adventurer, is passionate about continuous personal growth for both herself and others.
www.goldstars.com

contributors

Peggy Lee Hanson mentors those who experience life-changing situations. As owner of Personal Transition Guidance, LLC, she guides individuals through their journey using proven strategies, compassion, and support.
www.inspiration4Encouragement 2SupportU.com

Quin R. Hasler lives in Beltrami, Minnesota, with her parents and younger brother. She is in seventh grade and attends Fertile-Beltrami High School. Her hobbies include writing, reading, drawing, basketball, band, and choir. She is writing a book and is excited to be a published author.

Angela Harris lives near Washington, D.C., and enjoys having access to the many different cultures the city embraces. Her mentor and dear friend encouraged her to share her writings with others, making this her first published story.

JoAnne Hassen has written poems since elementary school. Her humorous poetry is featured at weddings, anniversaries, bachelorette parties, and other special events. Each December she mails a Christmas poem describing her family's year.

Jody Hauge and Jim have been married for forty-one years and raised three children. She enjoys cuddling with her nine beautiful grandchildren. Her faith has been her constant companion. She loves to travel, seek adventure, and spend time at their lake home, surrounded by family and friends.

A nurse for twenty-five years, **Cynthia J. Hickman** is pursuing a Ph.D. in health services. Recipient of numerous awards, she presents for local and national nursing organizations. To increase awareness of caring for others and giving back, she founded the Cynthia J. Hickman Pay It Forward Nursing Scholarship.

Trina Janson is mom to two children, two dogs, and one fur-ball cat. Married for eight years to her best friend (who is tolerant of her live-outside-the-box motto), she loves to spend time at the beach and cook gourmet meals. She always has a romance novel in tow.

For over thirty years, author and speaker **Janie Jasin, CSP,** has delivered wise words and laughter to audiences of teens, families, seniors, associations, healthcare professionals, and corporate moguls. Her books include *Traditions… Yeah, Yeah, Yeah! What's Your "Polka"?* and *The Littlest Christmas Tree* (one million sold). www.janiespeaks.com

Ellen Javernick enjoys two careers. By day she teaches kindergarten in Loveland, Colorado, and in the wee hours of the night she writes. Her newest books, published by Marshall Cavendish, are *The Birthday Pet* and *What If Everybody Did That?* She hopes she can inspire her ten grandchildren as much as her grandmother inspired her.

Married twenty-eight years, **Arlene Johnson** is the mother of six. Her family wages a battle with cancer in their lives. She is a physical therapist who feels honored to work with special needs children.

contributors

Janel Kresl and her husband Bill are the parents of teenagers, Brandon and Morgan. Janel teaches students with special education needs. In her spare time, she enjoys scrapbooking, reading, singing, and spending time with family and friends.

Lori LaBey is founder of Alzheimer's Speaks, an advocacy group providing education and support for people with early memory loss, as well as their families and professional care partners. Her mission is to shift caregiving from crisis to comfort.
www.AlzheimersSpeaks.com

Momma Joyce Lest is a woman who loves God and imparts the brotherhood of mankind to everyone she meets. She has a passion to serve and ease burdens, one person at a time.

Julie Rao Martin, of Boston, has launched a successful advertising career, an Internet start-up, and her business, Create-A-Stir. She co-wrote her first book with her beautiful daughter. Julie owes her passion and commitment to her phenomenal mother, Pauline.
www.create-A-Stir.com

Ann Martinka is the mother of three better-than-average children and wife to one better-than-average husband in Eden Prairie, Minnesota. In addition to managing their household, she works for Hammer Travel, providing travel opportunities for adults with developmental disabilities.

Dr. Susan Mathison, the "Holistic Cosmetic Surgeon," is a board-certified physician, mother, business owner, teacher, speaker, artist, writer, philanthropist, and part-time farm wife. She created PositivelyBeautiful to empower women to build a lifestyle that supports them in a journey toward balance in mind, body and spirit.
www.positivelybeautiful.com

Lisa McLeod-Lofquist is an attorney in Bloomington, Minnesota. A mother of four, she spent sixteen years in Alexandria, Minnesota, where she owned both a bookstore and a hockey team. Lisa is a graduate of St. Cloud State University and Hamline University School of Law.

An active volunteer, **Kay Miller** enjoys entertaining friends and family. She loved to travel with husband Phil and continues to find new adventures parasailing in Mexico, helicoptering over Hawaii, cruising Alaska, and roaming Europe. Kay spends quality time with her grandchildren fishing, hitting golf balls, and even mushroom hunting.

Marsha Miller has a successful public relations and consulting business. She writes and publishes for UPM, Inc., a global paper company. Marsha enjoys spending time with her husband John Chell and their daughter Kate. Gravity and menopause give chase, but she keeps a fast pace, hoping they'll give up!

contributors

Connie Nelson devoted her career years to special education. Passionate about her faith, she is still ministering to others. A devoted wife, mother, and grandmother of five, Connie makes her home in northwestern Minnesota along one of Minnesota's scenic lakes.

Sherry Staff Nelson, a married mother of two energetic boys, lives in Roseau, Minnesota, where she has been a sixth grade English teacher for more than twenty years. She believes that life is what you make of it, so enjoy the journey and live it to the fullest.

Carol McAdoo Rehme believes women friends pick you up, prop you up, and lift you up. A nationally award-winning author and editor, she publishes prolifically in the inspirational market. Her newest release, *Finding the Pearl*, recounts one spirited woman's rise from tragedy to triumph, from victim to victor.
www.rehme.com

Born in Butte, Montana, **Janice N. Richards** has a B.S. in secondary education with endorsements in special education, reading, and music. She taught for forty years before retiring in Rupert, Idaho, where her cats and two sons live. She continues writing and publishing.

Betsy A. Riley spends her days helping to make the world a better place, using science and technology and supercomputers through her job with the federal government. Evenings and weekends, she uses her talents in writing and artwork to spread joy and hope.
www.brws.com

Minnesota native **Judy Roelofs** traveled the country for her husband's work, planting deep roots in each community. She is an active volunteer, a faithful friend, and an inspiration to her grandchildren. Judy is a beloved second mom to Reneé Rongen.

Seventeen-year-old **Elizabeth (Bitsy) Rongen** loves adventure, friends, sports, animals, and shopping. She is a free spirit and an active volunteer, kind-hearted and rooted in faith. Bitsy plans to attend college and hopes for a career in pediatric healthcare.

Grace Rongen, fourteen, is passionate about sports. She plays basketball and volleyball and conquers the high waves on her wakeboard. Grace loves to laugh. She adores kids, babysitting, and hanging with friends. She volunteers her time and energy at many events.

Nancy Runstedler, Ontario, Canada, lives with a beautiful daughter and an overflowing book collection. She spends her days in libraries sharing her love of reading. She is a writer and huge supporter of the Pay It Forward Foundation. Helping others makes her happiest.

An instructor, healer, and mother, **Marina Semerikov** promotes breath and body awareness through yoga and the miracle ball method. She celebrates the essence of femininity with her three daughters. Originally from Oregon, Marina is a world traveler and global citizen.
www.marinawellnessandmassage.com

contributors

Tonya Sheridan is a life coach, writer, and founder of Lifestyle & Longevity LLC. Her philosophy is: When women go within and nurture their interior world, their exterior world takes care of itself.
www.TonyaSheridan.com

Born Kathleen Kelley to a Cherokee/Irish family of musicians and entertainers, **Kitty Sutton** performed in a one-woman show as Kitty Kelley in Branson, Missouri, for twelve years. *Wheezer and the Painted Frog* is Kitty's debut novel. She lives with her husband and three Jack Russell terriers.

LeAnn Thieman shares life lessons gleaned from the Vietnam Orphan Airlift. She authored *Balancing Life in Your "War Zones"* and twelve *Chicken Soup for the Soul* books. A Hall of Fame speaker, she motivates people to care for themselves as they care for others and make a difference.
www.LeAnnThieman.com

Tammy Tobin, born and raised in Ontario, Canada, moved to Australia in 2000. Armed with the lessons she has accrued, she is on a spiritual path to reconnect with her authentic self and live a life of service to mankind.

Nancy Clark Townsend was a New Yorker most of her life and now lives in Louisiana. She studied creative writing at Empire State College. Writing is her lifelong hobby. She is editor/writer for her church newsletter and belongs to two on-line writing groups, Advanced Writing Workshop and AARP's Writing Memoir.

Astra Türk is a spirited, twenty-eight-year-old, Estonian mother of three. She is the wife of one very lucky man.

Michelle Turnberg is a single mom, award-winning journalist, avid runner, and friend. A graduate of Concordia College and Minnesota State University Moorhead, she was a news anchor for fifteen years. Michelle writes for the Fargo Forum and is a professional speaker. She is training to run her ninth marathon.

Sharon Wall is a wife, mom, sister, grandmother, and cancer survivor who loves life. Her favorite pastimes are spending special moments with her children and grandchildren on Steamboat Lake. She is Reneé Rongen's mother!

Dawn Woods lives in Pierre, South Dakota, with her husband and son. She is the author of the children's book, *The Best Day Ever!*

artists

artists

artists

artists

artists

artists